WALES OFF MESSAGE

For Edward Tomos

WALES OFF MESSAGE

FROM CLAPHAM COMMON TO CARDIFF BAY

Patrick Hannan

seren

seren
is the book imprint of
Poetry Wales Press Ltd
Nolton Street, Bridgend, Wales
www.seren-books.com

© Patrick Hannan, 2000

The right of Patrick Hannan to be identified as the Author
of this Work has been asserted in accordance with the
Copyright, Designs and Patents Act 1988

ISBN 1-85411-293-7

A CIP record for this title is available from
the British Library

All rights reserved. No part of this publication
may be reproduced, stored in a retrieval system,
or transmitted at any time or by any means
electronic, mechanical, photocopying, recording
or otherwise without the prior permission
of the copyright holder.

*The publisher works with the financial assistance of the
Arts Council of Wales*

Printed in Plantin by CPD Wales, Ebbw Vale

CONTENTS

Acknowledgements	6
Naming the Names	7
Introduction	9
1: Ron Looks for Some Space	14
2: Rhodri Tidies His Sock Drawer	36
3: George Lends a Hand	50
4: Alun Is Returned to Sender	65
5: Rod Meets a Girl in a Pub	84
6: Redwood Gets Romantic	103
7: Prince Charles Has A Word With God	116
8: Sir Tasker and Sir Geoffrey Tackle the Gender Issue	132
9: Nick Uses a Rude Word	143
Postscript	157

Acknowledgements

A number of people who have discreetly helped me with this book would be appalled at the idea of having their contributions publicly advertised. They know who they are and how grateful I am to them. I also owe a great deal to the informal contributions of colleagues, politicians and friends with whom I have discussed various ideas and events and who have frequently stopped me getting things wrong. In particular I must thank Huw Roberts, Rhodri Morgan, Alun Michael and Peter Hain for the time they gave me. As will be obvious, none of them made any attempt to influence what I wrote or how I wrote it. I have included some quotations from the television series *Scandals* which I wrote and narrated for HTV Wales. I'm grateful to the production company, Fulmar West, and HTV Wales, for permission to use it. I have also made use of some material I wrote for the BBC Wales television series, which I made with Element Productions and which was due to be transmitted late in 2000. Penny Fishlock read the proofs unblinkingly and with her usual unerring eye for error and inconsistency. My wife, Menna, was unfailingly supportive, both in her practical approach to the text and in her deep understanding of the world it tries to describe. No Menna, no book.

Naming the Names

The great Welsh surname famine has a number of consequences of which the best known is the national inventiveness with nicknames. It's a useful way of distinguishing, for example, one Davies from another, but it's also the case that it has led to the practice of referring to prominent figures in public life by their first names. So it is that Ron and Rod and Alun and Rhodri are instantly identifiable, as they would not be if you said Davies, Richards, Michael or Morgan. It is a system that has now been enshrined in the conduct of the proceedings of the national assembly. There are some variations: Dafydd Wigley is often referred to as Wigley in private conversation because his second name is more distinctive than his first. Other people frequently seem to have both their names attached to them: Mike German, for instance, or Nick Bourne. I have adopted the custom in this book for the purposes of clarity rather than to imply any particular familiarity or disrespect.

Introduction

There is in Wales a capacity for comedy that reveals itself in unexpected ways. Frequently it fulfils the classic definition of humour, the gulf that often appears between aspiration and performance, the pompous man slipping on a banana skin. Who could have forecast, for example, the cheap fun the national assembly would provide in such abundance? Or again, surely only someone with a heart of stone could stifle the mirth provoked so frequently, and apparently inadvertently, by the Welsh Rugby Union. And our appreciation is intensified by the fact that the WRU itself doesn't get the joke.

Perhaps it's a sign of the times and of changing fashion that there are now people going round the world falsely claiming to be Welsh, but in the case of rugby this implied compliment has proved to be a serious embarrassment. In March 2000 it was revealed that two New Zealanders, both successful members of the Welsh national side, shouldn't actually have been playing at all. Shane Howarth and Brett Sinkinson were supposed to be qualified because they each had a Welsh grandparent – the minimum nationality requirement. They did not. Not only that, but no-one had thought to ask them for documentary evidence of any kind.

In the world scheme of things this isn't really very much by way of a disaster. Whoops, there goes the WRU again. More than that, you might think it showed a refreshing echo of the amateur spirit that once characterised the game. It was about trust and sportsmanship and higher human values rather than some bureaucratic investigation of rules and documents. Or, you might say, about people bumbling along in a fairly haphazard way. Howarth and Sinkinson had made an honest mistake. It is also perfectly understandable, particularly if you reverse the situation and you consider the chances of someone from Wales giving a single accurate answer about the geography of New Zealand. Sinkinson thought his grandfather had been born in Carmarthen when in fact it was in Oldham. As it happens, there are parts of Oldham from which you can see the

North Wales coast. If the rules had been slightly less tightly framed, so that anyone with a grandparent born *within sight* of Wales was eligible, there would have been no opportunity for the legalistic unravelling of the Welsh team that took place.

Besides, this wasn't really a Welsh problem. They were all at it. Scotland had a similar embarrassment with a New Zealander. There were Tongans playing for New Zealand, Australians playing for Japan and so on. In these circumstances I have a great deal of sympathy for the person who, in one of those man-in-the-street radio interviews at this time, said: "I think if you are of a Welsh persuasion then you should be considered Welsh".

Over the years we've become used to the fissures that sometimes open up unexpectedly between the WRU and real life. The question of eligibility was simply another of those treasured moments where, as in the traditional comic strip, someone had left the manhole cover off as the fat man walked obliviously towards it. Except for the fact that there was one aspect of this affair that had wider significance.

In the years from 1997 in particular, but for some decades before that, the question of what it was to be Welsh had been asked with increasing insistence. It was both a sign of political change and a consequence of it. As specifically Welsh institutions took root, so people were obliged to consider the broad cultural issue: what are the qualities and characteristics that distinguish Welsh people from everyone else in the world? Not language, certainly, except in the narrow sense that most people probably have a view on the Welsh language, for or against. Not race, although some people would try to persuade you that to be Welsh is to belong to a distinct racial group. Not a common enemy: the small numbers who enjoy romancing about English oppression down the centuries don't attract many subscribers.

Which brings us to sport. Now, you don't have to have any knowledge of rugby or soccer, what skills are required for playing them, or even what the rules are, to hold passionate views about the fortunes of the national sides. Chief amongst them is an unshakeable belief in the malign nature of a fate which makes Welsh teams lose so often. Second only to that is the conviction that, next time, it'll be different. These two games in particular evoke a patriotism that's not matched so unreservedly and universally in any other area of Welsh life. Even those whose hearts sink at the triumphalism victory so often brings still don't want Wales to lose.

There are a number of reasons why this is particularly true of rugby. One is the fact that, although it is increasingly widely played, it is not a world game in the sense that soccer is. So Wales can aspire to, sometimes even achieve, world status within rugby. It is also the case that for many people rugby teams have reinforced a sense of community. In their turn those communities have been represented in the greater unity of the Welsh side. It is also sometimes presented as a way in which the Welsh working class was able to assert its qualities, a method by which some of the oppressed could achieve fame and admiration and, particularly in recent years, economic freedom.

There's a great deal of mythology in all this, the miner changing from his pit clothes into the scarlet jersey of Wales and going out to score a try against England. There were always plenty of middle class grammar school boys in the Welsh team, for instance. But there's enough truth in it to make it a significant influence in the image of Wales. And, even in parts of Wales where rugby is very much a minority interest, it still grips people on those tumultuous international days.

Now, though, both rugby and Wales have altered beyond recognition. Industrial and social change has swept over the communities that gave birth to the household names of previous generations: Barry, Gareth, Gerald and the rest of those who never needed surnames and who became folk heroes in the seventies. It's difficult to believe that ever again will someone put up a statue of a rugby player, as they have of Gareth Edwards, in a Cardiff shopping mall. It turned out to be a last gesture to a disappearing way of life.

Twenty years ago no-one would have dreamt that a player, happily equipped with a Welsh granny, would travel half way round the world to play rugby for Wales. Nor would anyone have asked him to. But professional sport imposes different priorities, and who can blame a young man, someone with perhaps a single outstanding talent, for making a decent profit from it while he can? At the same time selectors and coaches would be considered culpable if they ignored any legitimate way of achieving the success inevitably demanded in what has become a multi-million pound sport.

No-one thinks that any of those involved in the eligibility row, officials or players – were deliberately setting out to deceive anyone. Grannygate, as it came to be called in the media, was in the great cock-up tradition of Welsh sport. Nor is the ancestry game anything new. After all, Vinnie Jones, the fearsome Wimbledon footballer, played for the Welsh team after a thorough investigation of the public records in North Wales. As he explained it to me at the time: "They said you could go back to your grandfather and they declared me legible [sic]". Many years ago, too, an uncle of mine, who at one time was chairman of the London Irish rugby club, asked me to keep an eye out for any players who, while not good enough for Wales, might qualify for Ireland if you climbed far enough up their family trees.

What is significant about the event, though, is the fact that, as political change in particular makes us more aware of our Welshness, one of the most easily understood aspects of that identity is becoming less Welsh. The ties between rugby and place have been loosened; people travel widely to play for the club that will give them the best financial deal. New Zealanders come to Llanelli, Welsh players head for London or France. The Welsh dressing room begins to sound like an episode of some antipodean soap opera.

It's no good weeping into our beer over this. It's the way these things work and it will not reduce by a single notch the fervour with which the Welsh team are roared on when they run out at the Millennium Stadium. More than that, it's clear that if Welsh rugby doesn't adopt the same practices as everyone else its prospects of being a significant force in the game will be minimal.

It is nevertheless a paradox that this has happened at a time when Wales has in other ways been obliged to consider what its distinctive identity might be, to some extent, indeed, to invent or develop that identity in something of a hurry. More than that, it has had to undergo the process in the glare of unexpected dramas and sensations.

Introduction

Above all, the events of the sixteen months between Ron Davies's politically fatal stroll on Clapham Common and Alun Michael's enforced resignation from the job of assembly First Secretary had an irresistible narrative drive. We were impatient for the next episode, taken unawares by twists in the story, absorbed by the human frailty of the chief characters and, at the end, felt a sense of satisfaction as the threads were pulled together in a logical denouement.

Compelling though all this was in itself, it also illustrated vividly the way in which Wales had changed. Now the country had its own political structure for the first time in history, it was necessary to consider what a specifically Welsh response to it might be. In particular it demanded a fresh examination of relationships between Wales and the rest of the United Kingdom. The circumstances in which Alun Michael was, in effect, sent back to London showed how testing and controversial those relationships might be for both sides.

I think it's only when you stand back and take an analytical look at the period that took Wales so unexpectedly from Ron Davies to Rhodri Morgan that you get any sense of the underlying pattern of events and the wider significance they might have. That is why, in this book, I have attempted to give an account of them and to consider some of the more tantalising questions they raise.

I suspect that in the end they will turn out to be more important than rugby.

1. Ron Looks for Some Space

It was thanks to an extraordinary and inexplicable act committed on October 27, 1998, that Ron Davies rightly earned a place in British political history. He then became the first Cabinet Minister ever to resign for not having done anything wrong. It was an unprecedented culmination to a series of bizarre events which had begun during the previous evening. Peter Hain, then a Welsh Office Minister, was to describe it as the second most surreal day in his entire life, outranked only by the occasion in 1975 when, the target of a campaign by the South African security service, BOSS, he was charged with robbing Barclays Bank in Putney. John Sergeant, in 1998 the BBC's Chief Political Correspondent, now Political Editor of ITN, manoeuvred by Downing Street into being Ron's sole interviewer that day, read the resignation letter with disbelief. "I said there's nothing in here that implies a resignation." On Radio Wales between five o'clock and half past six I interviewed a long queue of politicians, none of whom could hazard a coherent explanation for what had happened. It was soon being described as a scandal, but no-one could say of what the scandal consisted. An innocent man had apparently leapt on to the gallows and pulled the lever to open the trap door.

The story Ron had to tell was a simple one although, as time went on, it became clear that there were discrepancies in it. Indeed, it eventually seemed to consist more or less entirely of discrepancies but, given the imperfection of people's memories, particularly when they're in the grip of strong emotions, that didn't mean it wasn't true. Or largely true, anyway.

On the afternoon of Monday, October 26, he had driven himself back from Cardiff to his flat in Battersea. The demands of office were particularly oppressive at that stage and he'd forgone his summer holiday to campaign against Rhodri Morgan for the Welsh Labour leadership, a contest he'd finally won the previous month. A 'bruising' campaign was to become the journalistic shorthand for that period. Huw Roberts, who was Ron's political adviser, described the pressures of those long summer months on the road.

"It was an absolute killer. You're trying to run a country, you're trying to prepare for devolution. You have every department in Whitehall against you and he and I are running from one end of Wales to the other, facing constituency parties where Rhodri had been working on the ground for eighteen months. It was a killer. It was unbelievable.

"You'd have a day hammering away in a Cabinet committee with the English national party – which is what the Home Office is. You'd have days of meetings on apparently minor matters like whether you should call someone a prime minister or a first secretary. You'd come away, shoot down here, jump in the car, drive to Aberystwyth, find that Rhodri and about twenty of his mates were in the room already, and then drive back. We were dead."

That was how Ron had spent a good part of the summer and he was decidedly rattled. I bumped into him in the BBC newsroom in Cardiff during August and asked some inane and ill-advised question about him enjoying his holidays. He gave me a series of V-signs and shouted, "Fuck off, fuck off, fuck off". After all this and all the regular and unceasing demands of just being a minister, that day in October he needed some space, he said. To get it he'd decided to go for a walk on Clapham Common. What happened then he described briefly in his letter of resignation.

"Whilst walking, I was approached by a man I had never seen before who engaged me in conversation. After talking for some minutes he asked me to accompany him and two of his friends to his flat for a meal. We drove, in my car, to collect his friends, one male, one female. Shortly afterwards, the man produced a knife and together with his male companion robbed me and stole my car, leaving me standing at the roadside."

I think most people would agree that to go walking in the evening on Clapham Common, parts of which are notoriously the haunt of homosexuals, prostitutes and drug dealers, to fall into conversation with a total stranger, a Rastafarian, and to agree to go home with him can fairly be described as "a serious lapse of judgement", the phrase Ron was to use in his letter. Tony Blair's official spokesman made much the same point in a commendably restrained manner the next day. The *Daily Telegraph* reported: "...he said the Prime Minister shared Mr. Davies's view that it was a 'lapse of judgement' for a Cabinet Minister to meet a complete stranger in a London park and then drive around south London with him".

Even so, it's difficult to see why this event, later to become known as the 'moment of madness', was in itself a reason for Ron to make such an abrupt decision to resign as Secretary of State for Wales. Occasional foolishness, while frowned upon in modern Government, is not an automatic disqualification from office, and Ron's account of his adventures showed a rather touching innocence and *naïveté*, perhaps, deserving of no more than a brisk official lecture on the dangers of being too trusting. And whatever else has been said since, in all this Ron has consistently presented himself as a victim of another person's crime.

The next day other people began to worry away at the mystery. Why should someone, even a Cabinet Minister, have to resign because he's been robbed by a man carrying a knife in South London? Surely even having your mobile phone stolen, with all those confidential numbers in its memory, doesn't necessarily lead to political oblivion. When people began to look at the circumstances in this way, other views of the events were formed.

In the first place there was a distinct impression that Ron wanted to resign quickly and without spending too much time on the details of what had actually happened. Although his meeting with the Prime Minister lasted three quarters of an hour, it was clear that Ron had taken the initiative and was not inclined to discuss whether or not he should go. In the face of this attitude Tony Blair was hardly likely to attempt to persuade him to stay, although it emerged later that Downing Street itself was never entirely clear what exactly had led to Ron's decision. The immediate task for officials was what the spin doctoring trade calls damage limitation. Ron couldn't really be spirited away without a word, but at the same time he could hardly be exposed to the unfenced safari park of a Westminster press conference. The decision was made that he'd give one, pooled, interview, to be made available to all the broadcasting organisations, and then a last, secret trip in the ministerial car to meet his wife and daughter at a Center Parc in Wiltshire.

During the afternoon John Sergeant got a phone call at the BBC offices in Millbank asking him to go to Number Ten to interview the Prime Minister about the economy. Come over quickly, he was urged. After thirty years in the trade Sergeant isn't in awe of anybody. He wasn't sure he wanted to interview the Prime Minister about the economy but this sort of invitation, half a request, half an implied instruction, is difficult to refuse. Something important might just happen.

In Downing Street he was met by Godric Smith, deputy to the Prime Minister's official spokesman, Alastair Campbell. "He said the interview wasn't at Number 10, it was at the Welsh Office," Sergeant recalled later. "I thought it was odd and I was a bit fed up. I wondered if I was being manipulated in some way."

To be frank, senior Westminster political correspondents wouldn't dream of setting foot in the Welsh Office unless it were for a totally sensational story (and nothing of that nature had been known to arise at any time since the department was first established in 1951) or perhaps, briefly, for a free drink at Christmas. Well, there's always a first time for everything and sensational story it turned out to be, although Sergeant was unable to work out immediately why that should be so.

He was escorted across Whitehall to Gwydyr House, the Welsh Office's London headquarters. He was told that Ron had resigned and was handed the letter he had written to the Prime Minister. He had about a minute and a half to work out what the reasons were, but the correspondence was decidedly unhelpful. As was Ron himself when he came in to be interviewed, relaxed enough to try a little joke – "We've finally got you to the Welsh Office," he said.

"He sat down and he started not telling me what he hadn't done on Clapham Common," Sergeant said. There were plenty of questions to be asked but no attempt by Ron to answer them, to amplify in any way exactly what it was about his behaviour that had led him to be so resolute in his determination to resign. Sergeant describes his own mood at this stage as being truculent, particularly as he was having misgivings about his role in what was clearly some kind of attempted fix by Downing Street. For that reason it became a more difficult interview than he thought it need otherwise have been. Since Ron wasn't giving very much away, Sergeant had to do most of the work.

That included, inevitably, asking the question that had leapt into most people's minds as soon as they heard even a rough outline of the story. Was the real background to this sexual? In fact, even before this interview had taken place, a visitor to Downing Street was told, as he went through the door, that Ron had resigned. When he asked why he was told: "A homosexual encounter on Clapham Common". Officials never repeated that publicly and Ron, in his interview with John Sergeant, denied it specifically.

"Isn't it enough to say that as a member of the Cabinet I am accepting that I was guilty of an error of judgement?" he continued, in a way which underlined his anxiety to get away from confronting the details of what had happened to him on the previous evening.

His central problem wasn't the question of whether his story was true or not. It just wasn't good enough. Not good enough, that is, for a public brought up on a daily diet of scandal fed by insistent journalists skilled at putting it on their breakfast tables. The trouble is that, from a journalistic point of view, life is often pretty unsatisfactory with all its rough edges, inexplicable events and unlikely coincidences spoiling the neat patterns into which reporters and editors like to describe the undeserved rise and inevitable fall of public figures of all kinds and conditions. This is a world in which no-one goes for a walk on Clapham Common in the evening except in pursuit of drugs, prostitutes or, most probably, gay sex. It would clearly be some time before the newspapers got bored with this story, however little Ron said about it and however accurate the minimal account he was willing to provide. His problem was that his tale didn't sound true, even if was a completely honest account (although rather lacking in any convincing corroborative detail) of what took place that night.

As often happens in these circumstances the world quickly divided into two groups: those who were astounded by what had happened and those who said they'd known all along. In the first category were at least two people who knew Ron well and who used strikingly similar terms when describing what they knew of his attitudes to sex. One of them was astonished when it was suggested that Ron was a homosexual.

"I just could not believe what they were saying. If anything he tended to be a bit leery towards women. He was a bit unreconstructed in that. Not exactly a new man, although he was very supportive of women in terms of appointments."

Another colleague said very much the same: "He could be old-fashionedly politically incorrect in his attitudes to some of the girls in the office. I have to say that I have never seen anything that suggested he had a homosexual aspect to his character."

Even so, within minutes of the resignation being made public and some of the circumstances behind it becoming clear, there were plenty of people who announced that there had always been rumours and they'd been hearing them for years, of sexual adventures on various pieces of open ground around Machen, near Caerphilly, where Ron lived. Civil servants, party workers and journalists gleefully exchanged gossip, sometimes with places, dates and times apparently giving authenticity to the stories. But it's always important to be careful about evidence, much of it hearsay, that emerges after the event. I've certainly heard detailed allegations about other prominent people in Wales who'd been disgraced in some way or another: importuning, indecency, drunken driving, being over-persistent with girls who kept saying no, low-grade sinning in the main. You are almost invariably told that not only were these transgressions widely known, but that their perpetrators had been warned by police to cease their various activities in public lavatories and other places, or face the consequences. If I'd been told these things before these people were arrested, rather than after the event, I'd have been more impressed. It's also the case that the police value the publicity and deterrent value attached to arresting minor celebrities for even more minor crimes. In recent times in Wales bishops, judges and members of parliament have been dragged through the courts for sad little adventures in public places. There has been no sign of reluctance on the part of the authorities to prosecute them.

Well, whatever Ron had or hadn't done on Clapham Common the consequences were abrupt. He was out of Cabinet and back in the bus queue. But there was another problem to be resolved. He had resigned as Secretary of State for Wales but he was still the Labour Party's Welsh leader and, as such, would automatically become First Secretary of the assembly when, as was generally assumed, his party formed the administration after the elections the following May. Some people speculated that officials in Downing Street, including the Prime Minister himself, had been so taken aback by the events of the day and Ron's almost indecent haste to resign and disappear, that they hadn't asked him about his intentions in this matter. That they had indeed entirely forgotten about the Welsh assembly and his role in it. It's possible: the minders and spin doctors have, as we'll see, a rather more inflated reputation for efficiency and control than the record would seem to bear out.

The next day some people believed that, despite everything, Ron would be able to continue with the Welsh job. Leighton Andrews, a leading campaigner for a 'Yes' vote in the 1997 referendum and who, as a political consultant, is supposed to be a good judge of such things, said he thought Ron could still be First Secretary. It seemed unlikely. The Clapham Common incident was bound to be thrown at him every day. Journalists would trawl through his dustbins and lie in wait for him wherever he went. (They did a great deal of that anyway, as it turned out.) Opponents would sneer that someone who wasn't good enough for the Cabinet was nevertheless considered good enough by the Labour Party to be its most senior politician in Wales. In the long campaigning months between October and May it would form the most important single item on the political agenda. It was difficult to think his continuing would be anything but a disaster for the Welsh Labour Party although, it transpired later, it was an organisation perfectly capable of manufacturing plenty of others to take its place.

Another associate of Ron's considered that, despite those difficulties, he could have continued if he'd made a frank statement about the events of October 26 and about his own sexuality: in other words, if he'd 'come out'. But his version was that there was nothing to come out about. He was the victim of an unpleasant crime who, because of who he was and what he did for a living, had paid a double penalty for a moment's inadvertence. It didn't take long for him to make the inevitable decision. On Thursday night he wrote to his constituency party in Caerphilly withdrawing from the leadership. He said, once again, that the events of the previous Monday would "haunt him for ever", while continuing his refrain that he had done "nothing improper or illegal".

The circumstances surrounding this second resignation were embarrassing enough for the Welsh Labour Party but the political consequences were to be much more damaging and long-lasting than anyone could have anticipated. Alun Michael, the Blair super-loyalist and Deputy Home Secretary, was made Secretary of State for Wales within an hour or so of Ron's first meeting in Downing Street. The following week he announced that he would be standing for the Welsh leadership. Rhodri Morgan would have a second go and would clearly be no pushover. The circus was on the road again.

As far as Ron was concerned he might have hoped this decision would have marked the end of serious interest in his private life. London newspapers are notoriously indifferent to what goes on in Wales and perhaps there wasn't much journalistic mileage left in the escapades of an ex-Cabinet minister and an ex-would-be First Secretary of a Welsh assembly that didn't even exist at this stage. Some things would remain unexplained, but soon enough they'd be wrapping chips. All that would be left would be that forlorn and meaningless obituary phrase, much used at the time, 'a personal tragedy', an expression that was even further devalued by its application a few months later to Peter Mandelson's irregular home loan.

But the newspapers hadn't lost interest. Even more curiously, it was at this point that Ron was to start invading his own privacy.

For a man who wasn't saying anything, Ron spent a great deal of time going round not saying it in the most public possible manner. On the Friday, four days after the events on Clapham Common, he drove to Cardiff to give interviews to Glyn Mathias of BBC Wales and Max Perkins of HTV. It was an unilluminating occasion, except for one thing. Written on the back of his hand in red ink was the word 'sorry'. Sorry for what? was the chorused response of the media and, in so far as it's possible to tell, the public. After all, he hadn't done anything wrong except make an error of judgement at a time of distraction.

"I can give you an absolute assurance that I was involved in no illegal behaviour, no improper behaviour whatsoever and the suggestion that there was that sort of behaviour is just not true."

Oh, come off it, Ron. Are you gay?

"I am not going to get into a position of answering that sort of question."

But in case you'd missed the point: "I have a very long-term, loving, stable relationship with my wife and she has been marvellously supportive of me during this week". Such statements, true or not, are the small change of the scandal rebuttal game, very much as other MPs like to be photographed with their loving families shortly after they've been the subject of bonk headlines of one kind or another. This is the sort of thing politicians do and it's not necessarily meant to be taken literally. Ron went on saying very much that sort of thing for some considerable time. Was he or wasn't he? The implication of his answer to Mary Riddell in the *Daily Mail* the following February seemed clear enough.

"You sense that Davies is haunted by some deeper denial. Surely he, a libertarian, sees no shame in being gay or bisexual."

"That is a matter for those individuals concerned. It doesn't apply to me... I'm not going to get involved in a detailed discussion of my sexuality. Why should I? Suffice it to say all the stuff I've seen written is rubbish."

To most people that would seem pretty unambiguous. The phrase "It doesn't apply to me" was about the clearest thing Ron had said up to that point about his sexual nature. Although he said he wasn't going to talk about it, if the simple English words mean anything they were a direct denial that he was gay or bisexual. The curious fact that he was discussing it in the same breath as saying he wouldn't discuss it was just another minor paradox in the whole business. End of story, then. Far from it.

Perhaps one of the most unexpected aspects of this affair,

especially for those who know the short attention span possessed by most journalists and editors, was that people went on with their inquiries long after you'd have thought the last remaining drop of juice had been squeezed from this particular lemon. For a number of reasons Ron proved to be a challenge to reporters who nagged away at all the unanswered questions long after they would normally have found a more up-to-date scandal. One reason almost certainly was that, under the Tories, they'd been provided with a sensation every week or so. Now they had to make the best of things at a time of a sleaze shortage.

That the *Daily Mail* was publishing an interview with Ron almost four months after the event was a clear indication of the continuing fascination of the case. The fact that he was giving such interviews showed his own ambiguity: he wanted privacy for himself and his family, he didn't want to confront the details of the events that led to his downfall, but at the same time he somehow had to keep talking about them. In March his face was on the cover of the *Sunday Times* magazine. Inside were six pages of sympathetic prose recounting the events of that tumultuous October week, an article clearly based on conversations with some of Ron's closest associates. This was quite extraordinary coverage of what was by now a stale story about a minor drama in the life of someone who, as a humiliated and out-of-office Welsh politician, was by definition a person of stupendous obscurity.

It was perhaps the unsatisfactory nature of the explanations so far, the journalistic instinct that there had to be more to it than that, that kept people on the trail. It had by now become a sort of detective story in the course of which Ron dropped a number of clues. The most specific of them came in the personal statement he made in the House of Commons on the afternoon of November 2. It was a week after the central incident and a day after some of the Sunday papers had published lurid allegations about his *al fresco* sex life. Thanks to the efficient services of the publicist Max Clifford, Ron's ex-wife had also joined in with her version of an erratic and colourful home life during the time their marriage lasted.

Later Ron and his friends said important parts of the statement had been ruled out of order by the Speaker, Betty Boothroyd, but much of it was a robust reply to the accusations made by the tabloids, which he described as "a stream of rubbish". There was, though, one passage in particular that persuaded many people that he was trying, cryptically, to indicate, without actually admitting it, that there was some truth in the allegations.

"We are what we are," he said. "We are all different, the products both of our genes and our experiences. Members of Parliament are no different from the society we represent."

That first phrase was considered to be particularly significant, echoing as it did, *I Am What I Am*, the Gloria Gaynor song which has been widely adopted as a gay anthem. It was a plea for tolerance reinforced by a reference to a painful childhood and the lesson it had taught him. "You can't allow powerful people to bully the weak or to abuse their own power. Not for the first time in my life I have been badly beaten and hurt. I believe my defences are strong enough to see me through this trying time."

But what exactly did this all mean? That became much clearer a little later in the day. He and his two brothers and sister had frequently been savagely beaten by their father. A television journalist to whom, some time before, he had described his experiences in confidence, was told that he could now make the information public. Later still, one of Ron's brothers gave interviews about what had happened nearly forty years before.

Well, there we were, then. You didn't have to be a code breaker down at MI6 to work out what this was all about. And who could fail to be sympathetic, to be moved even, by the life briefly revealed as a curtain was held back for a moment, and by the disproportionate penalty that had now been paid by someone who was now a victim of violence twice over?

But that wasn't the party line at all. Huw Roberts, who'd stayed close to him through the troubles, briefed the press that this was in no sense an admission that Ron was homosexual. And as time went on other interpretations were put on the words: that Ron's childhood had given him an independent assertiveness of spirit which might lead him into danger. And that his spirit had been so toughened by those experiences he would not be crushed by the emotional and physical pressures of his present difficulties. In particular he insisted later he wasn't suicidal, despite a less than tactful remark to journalists by Alastair Campbell that there were fears he might do himself some harm.

In any case, what did it all matter at this stage? Ron's career as a politician of any serious influence was apparently over and he was welcome to keep his secrets. People would think what they thought, snigger a bit, make some Clapham Common jokes until they found another target, and eventually push the story into the file of cautionary tales of politicians who got into trouble in unsavoury circumstances. But in fact Ron was by no means finished and his real downfall was yet to come, a consequence of the political rather than the sexual side of his nature.

When you ask people who have worked closely with him what kind of person Ron is, they are often unexpectedly hesitant. One politician said: "He's a much more complex character than anybody could see from the surface, partly because the valleys boy image was so comprehensive a shell that he looked one-dimensional when he was absolutely the reverse. He's a very complicated character but it's hidden away. His defining characteristic has to be his monumental insecurity, an absolute uncertainty of his right to be where he was.

"He's also the most un-crony-like person on earth. He does not make friends. It's been a huge problem for him. It's very hard to see any Ron crowd in the House of Commons, for instance. He earns respect, not love."

Another colleague made a similar assessment. "I wouldn't say he had any friends, personal friends. He had people who backed him and who were close supporters, but his support in the party was very ambivalent. He also had an enormous number of enemies which is why, when his fall came, it was so sharp. He just didn't have anyone to back him."

One thing everyone agrees on is that he is a very astute and determined politician. Those who saw him in his bad-tempered battles with Russell Goodway, the Leader of Cardiff City Council, over a headquarters for the assembly, felt he relished the conflict. He was also very rough on Llew Smith, the old-style Marxist MP for Blaenau Gwent who opposed devolution in any form. Llew, who is perfectly capable of looking after himself, accused Ron of threatening him. Ron affected bafflement, implying that he was the kind of person who would be thrown out of the Quakers for being too meek.

"He is one of the few people who can say to you face to face what is a total lie. What you *know* is a total lie," a Welsh MP said. "There's an odd combination of a visionary, inclusive, very astute, consummate politician, a modern politician in his attitudes towards participatory politics, towards involving women. He is very open-minded.

"But on the other side of it is this manipulative bully; devious, dishonest in many respects."

These, we should remember, are the words of a supporter.

That description might actually fit a hundred politicians, particularly politicians who've managed to get things done. It's not a trade for the squeamish or the over-scrupulous and a substantial part of the credit for there being an assembly at all is owed to Ron. Even more remarkable was his achievement in getting a system of proportional representation introduced for the assembly elections in the face of the Old Labour motto that inclusivity is for wimps.

Huw Roberts believes only Ron could have done it. "He's an operator, there's no doubt at all about that. He didn't seem to mind too much about how he was perceived as long as he got what he wanted. It's hard to imagine any other member of the Labour Party active in Wales who could have got the party to vote unanimously for a devolution proposal which contained an element of proportional representation."

In this, and in many of the things that have happened since, one characteristic emerges more strongly than any other: he is an obsessive. In the seventies, before he went into Parliament, Ron was part of the anti-devolution lobby. There were perfectly respectable arguments for taking that line and those who supported it might well have been a majority in the Labour Party in Wales in the period leading up to the disastrous referendum of March 1, 1979. Ron changed his mind, as did many others. After all, it returned to the party's agenda during the leadership regime of Neil Kinnock who, only a few years before, had himself been perhaps the single most influential figure in wrecking it. Indeed, people have changed their minds about many things – so much so that a Labour MP who today argues for public ownership is dismissed as a crank.

But Ron didn't simply alter his view. He embraced devolution with a rare passion, something that might be considered foolhardy in the light of the active hostility of many Welsh voters and the indifference of most of the rest. It became his project. When he lost control of it he became like the one-time owner of a treasured train set who had to look on appalled while a bunch of rough boys threatened to wreck it. But did he have to give it up for good, or could he grab it back?

Within the Labour Party in Wales there are a large number of influential people who think that, despite everything, Ron believed he could still be First Secretary of the national assembly: that he might, after all, have been the beneficiary of the electoral system he had persuaded his party to endorse. When, in February 1999, and in succession to Ron, Alun Michael won the election for the leadership of the Welsh Labour Party, there was still no guarantee that he would actually manage to be elected to the assembly itself. He hadn't put himself forward as a candidate for any of the constituencies and his late arrival on the scene, amid recriminations over what was portrayed as a London fix, no doubt persuaded him that that course would simply bring him a humiliating rebuff. Instead he had to rely on getting through as one of the twenty additional members provided for by the proportional representation system.

What that meant was that his political fate ultimately depended on Labour doing badly in the Mid and West Wales region where he was put at the top of the Labour list. The corrective mechanism of the system would work in his favour only as long as Labour didn't win too many of the individual seats in the area. What it boiled down to was that, in order for him to succeed, a decent proportion of his party colleagues had to fail. In particular he needed Plaid Cymru, the object of many of his most caustic comments during the campaign, to do well. We were now living in a political world where a leader's fate depended to some extent on his party losing rather than winning.

Ron calculated that Alun couldn't do it. What he told other people in the party indicated clearly that he believed the elaborate arithmetic of the election would keep Alun out of the assembly. There would therefore be a vacancy for First Secretary which would now be decided, not by the party-wide vote that had elected first him and then Alun, but jointly by the members of the assembly and the party's Welsh executive. Step forward Ron Davies, rehabilitated after that bit of trouble which was, after all, fading from the collective public consciousness. The man they liked to call the architect of devolution (and the man who liked to be called it), the man without whom there might not have been an assembly at all, could reclaim his rightful inheritance to the murmured approval of a party grateful for someone to get them out of the mess.

In the course of the election campaign he pressed fellow-candidates on what they would do if his predicted outcome occurred. Even on the day of the election itself he was telling people that Alun wouldn't be elected and that he, Ron, was the man to take his place. In the event, though, his calculations turned out to have gone badly wrong. Alun Michael did win a seat, thanks to Plaid Cymru's exceptionally good performance and Labour's poor one. In one of those curious paradoxes which were characteristic of these events, Labour's vote was adversely affected by, among other things, the opposition to the way in which Alun Michael had been chosen. So he remained leader thanks in substantial part to the fact that many people didn't want him to be leader.

Ron's hopes were dashed, but there was worse to come. He had virtually been promised, although not in so many words, a place in Alun Michael's Cabinet. Very late into that selection process, after the elections, Ron's was one of the names still on the preliminary list. Soon, though, it disappeared. Alun had telephoned all the Labour AMs with a list of questions, including one about their attitudes to Ron. At best there wasn't much enthusiasm. Some people thought that, despite everything, he could be an asset to an inexperienced administration. But others, resentful of his conduct during the election campaign, urged Alun to leave him out.

When the cabinet list was announced on April 12, Ron said

he was bitterly disappointed. "Alun didn't give me any explanation which I find credible." Given Ron's undisguised admiration for his own abilities it is in fact difficult to imagine an explanation he might have thought credible.

Alun said, as politicians do, that he thought Ron would play "a very significant and creative role" as an assembly member. He didn't go into any details as to how he thought that might be achieved.

Two days later a rumour swept through the Welsh political world that a disgruntled Ron was planning to join Plaid Cymru. The general view was that for its own sake Plaid Cymru would be well advised to tell him to stay where he was. A few hours after that it was announced that Ron was to be chairman of the assembly's economic affairs committee. It was recognition of a sort but, once again, it wasn't to last very long.

The Queen had hardly shaken the dust of Cardiff Bay off her shoes after the official opening of the assembly before the *News of the World* was back on the Clapham Common trail. In a two-page spread published on June 13, the paper accused Ron of trawling for gay sex in a woodland area near his home. The headline, over a number of explicit allegations about his behaviour, was in the great tabloid tradition: "This MP is a public menace".

Ron reacted even before the paper reached people's homes. Overnight he issued a statement in which he said he had been walking and bird-watching when he was approached by two men who tried to engage him in conversation of a sexual nature. This was clearly the work, he said, of tabloid journalists trying to entrap him.

But there was more, and it was rather more startling than anything the *News of the World* had written. He concluded: "I am left with no alternative but to confirm that I am, and have been for some time, bisexual". In some ways this admission was as much another puzzle as it was an explanation. Why did allegations which he insisted were false in every particular provoke him into making an admission which was bound to undermine much of what he had said over the previous eight months? It answered some questions but raised others. The following weekend he provided some more answers himself, this time in the

Welsh tabloid, *Wales on Sunday*.

Over four pages readers were able to learn something about Ron's private life, although not as much as appeared at first sight. "I am a sick man, says Ron Davies", was the confessional tone set by the front page, but the article itself was rather short on much that looked like facts. He was being treated for a psychiatric disorder, he told the reporter, Martin Shipton. He was someone with "a darker side" and, in Shipton's opinion, "it was clear that he has had sexual encounters with men".

He went on: "Over the past few months I have been coming to terms with the fact that there are inexplicable elements to some of my actions. Having come to terms with this and confronted it, I have therefore sought and have received professional help through the NHS. I now understand that I have a form of compulsive disorder which causes me to seek out high-risk situations... I have acknowledged that I am a bisexual. I have never had what most people would understand to be a gay relationship. All my primary feelings, both emotional and physical, have been towards women."

It's difficult, even now, to know what to make of this confession which went on to explain that his dedication to the cause of devolution was merely the other, positive, side of a character which led him into the dark places of experiment and danger. But I suppose you can't really expect someone publicly announcing such distressing details about his private life to be particularly coherent.

A central question remained: what about the events on Clapham Common the previous October? What was he really doing there?

He repeated the story he had always told, the culmination of stress, distraction, the need for a period of calm. But reflection and treatment suggested to him that his motives might not have been as unambiguous as he had hitherto believed. *Wales on Sunday* reported:

"He said he was intrigued at the prospect of going with unknown company, male and female, for a drink, a meal and perhaps to watch a video in unknown and strange surroundings. With hindsight, and in the light of the greater understanding Mr. Davies has gained, he now realises there was, perhaps, a sexual undercurrent, but nothing explicit, and he is adamant that in the event nothing of a sexual nature occurred."

There is absolutely no obligation on anyone to make sense when they describe and explain their actions and motives. So while some people might think that Ron, threatened with exposure, was telling the Welsh public as little as he could get away with in the circumstances, others might accept that he had now acquired a genuine insight into his emotional condition which provided a rational explanation for what until then had been an inexplicable piece of behaviour.

You might also think that the diagnosis provided by an unnamed therapist (and how arresting it is that political correctness made him emphasise that the treatment was being provided by the National Health Service, even if it was at "one of Britain's top specialist clinics") that he had a disorder that compelled him to seek out dangerous situations, was just so much psychobabble. But there are parallel cases which perhaps lend this explanation some authenticity.

Following the death of John F. Kennedy Jr. in an air crash in July that year, Alexander Chancellor reported in his column in the *Guardian* weekend magazine: "Israeli molecular geneticist, Dr. Richard Ebstein, claimed that the Kennedys have a rare gene, the D-4 receptor and serotonin transporter gene which he has discovered and which makes people impulsive and given to taking chances".

So there we are. It is a disease, it has an identifiable cause and it has a history and, in its way, it has a certain amount of glamour. It also goes some way towards explaining, as he did himself, that Ron's political and sexual character are of a piece, and that there is a dangerously compulsive element in him which leads him to do things others wouldn't. It's hardly necessary to add that Ron had some considerable way to go in all aspects of his life before he could be bracketed with the Kennedys.

As far as the sexual aspect was concerned, the Welsh public was allowed only a short summer break before we were once again plunged into another aspect of a subject about which perhaps we already knew more than enough. In August Ron announced that he and his wife, Christina, were to divorce.

Early in September the lead story in *Wales on Sunday* shrieked: "Ron's 'love' Rumpus".

Tireless reporters had tracked down the former Welsh Secretary to the Cliff Hotel in Gwbert-on-Sea, on the Cardiganshire coast, and discovered him there with a woman. Ron was interviewed by the paper and he explained that there was nothing scandalous about the association. Both he and his companion were separated from their spouses and, please note, they were occupying separate rooms. The excitability of *Wales on Sunday* can be gauged from the fact that it described the Cliff as a 'top' hotel, although anyone who has ever been there would tell you that the only place it might possibly be a top hotel is in Gwbert-on-Sea, although it is, admittedly, a *cliff*-top hotel.

Continuing his habit of living dangerously, Ron provided the next day's *Western Mail* with an interview and thus its lead story, the headline of which sprawled across seven columns. "Lynne, my close friend and rock", it said, revealing that Ron and Lynne Hughes, 33, met at a Welsh language course in Aberystwyth. Ron said: "We have a perfectly proper and innocent relationship". Lynne herself was chiefly upset about one thing. She didn't like being described in the papers as a brunette because she thought it made her sound like "some sort of bimbo".

Ron's political career meanwhile, diminished though it was, had been even further emasculated by his confession of bisexuality. He maintained his chairmanship of the economic development committee until the end of June. But at a session in which the committee questioned the First Secretary, Alun Michael, there were particularly bad-tempered exchanges which many observers believed had their origin in Ron's belief in his superior knowledge and talents; in particular in his conviction that he ought to be sitting where Alun was sitting. His colleagues had had enough, even if he hadn't, and shortly afterwards Ron announced he was resigning the chairmanship – "for the good of the party".

Even in these circumstances, however, he was unabashed. If one political career closed then he'd simply invent another. This time it was as keeper of the holy flame of devolution. As early as July, *Wales on Sunday* reported that he was disillusioned with the way in which Alun Michael was conducting the affairs of the national assembly. He wasn't quoted directly but in the light of what was to come some months later a pattern was already beginning to emerge.

In December he was once again confiding his thoughts to *Wales on Sunday*, criticising Alun for the way in which he was running things, particularly because of his "take it or leave it attitude" towards other parties when presenting policy. In January, in a letter to his constituency party, which was unaccountably leaked to the press, he commended Plaid Cymru's attitude towards Treasury funding to match potential European grants through the Objective One system (of which rather too much later) while describing Labour's efforts as "inept".

It began to get like old times in the Labour Party, where they have long reserved their most passionate hatreds for each other. Over the next few days people stopped speaking in code. Someone described as "a senior Labour source" said that "[Ron] cannot accept that he threw away the leadership of the assembly and that the party does not want him back".

Alun Michael joined in patronisingly by saying: "[Ron] appears to have lost touch with the complex nature of the issue".

Ron responded a couple of days later: "I was one of the few potential leadership candidates to openly support Alun Michael, but that does not mean I shall suspend my critical faculties". (More accurately, when he supported Alun he was actually an ex-potential leadership candidate and, moreover, an ex-leader, but let's not start being finicky at this stage.)

The next day he was quoted as saying he was disappointed that personal and public abuse had crept into Labour's political debate. Hardly had he spoken than Jackie Lawrence, Secretary of the Welsh group of Labour MPs, said that Ron seemed to be "treacherous and untrustworthy".

This would have been extraordinary enough in any circumstances, but this naked ill-feeling was being paraded through Wales at a time when Labour, a minority administration in the assembly after all, was on the verge of the humiliating prospect of Alun Michael being pushed out of office altogether. In these difficult circumstances would Ron be insensitive enough to make matters worse? There was no need to hold your breath. He might as well have had seventy-six trombones to lead him into the lecture he was to give to the Institute of Welsh Governance on the evening of January 19, such was the anticipation that had been so carefully built up. This was Ron the dispassionate analyst, Ron the big thinker, the man who had worked with pick and shovel at the coal face of constitutional change, pointing out deficiencies in a system which he was better qualified than anyone to judge. It was just unfortunate that his duty to speak out happened to involve a comprehensive rubbishing of his own party and its leadership.

He had already announced that he now believed that the assembly should have the power to legislate and raise taxes, a considerable change from the scheme he had so passionately commended to Welsh voters only a couple of years previously. Now, anyway, the whole thing was falling apart.

"We cannot go on as we are," he said, "limping on, day to day, issue by issue."

Luckily, though, he also had a five-point plan to rescue the whole affair, the details of which need not concern us here. The core of what was essentially an attack on his own party was contained in a single sentence. "Labour must make it clear that we view the assembly as the Cardiff headquarters of Welsh government and not the Cardiff branch office of London headquarters."

If you had drawn up a list of the most unhelpful things he could have said, this would have been at the top of it. Alun Michael had long been portrayed by political opponents and the press as a man who had been parachuted into the assembly to take his orders direct from Labour's centralised Millbank machine. It was at the heart of the attacks being made on him by the opposition parties. Now Ron, the high priest of the cult of devolution, had pronounced his unfavourable judgement. It could only end in tears, and, just over a fortnight later, it did.

I wouldn't argue for a second that Ron's public attacks on Labour and its leader (by clear implication if not so much by name) was the decisive factor in what was to follow. But his views and the publicity he sought for them did help give some legitimacy to a manoeuvre the other parties tried to drape in the robes of principle. And although his was an extreme view of the assembly's failings, there's no doubt that he reflected in his own way the opinions of Alun held rather more discreetly by a substantial number of the other members of the Labour group. But in all this there's perhaps nothing more remarkable than Ron's story itself. When you look at it as a narrative you realise that his survival as a public figure has been miraculous. His resilience is astonishing, his ability, despite a catalogue of disasters, to carry on as if nothing very much has occurred, almost unbelievable. His career illustrates the truth that almost anything can happen in politics and I would not rule out almost anything happening to Ron in the future.

Chutzpah is sometimes defined as the quality enjoyed by the man who, having murdered his father and his mother, asked the court for mercy on the grounds that he was an orphan. On the day Alun Michael resigned as First Secretary, I bumped into Ron in the excited crowd in the milling area of the assembly building. No decision had been made about Alun's successor. "Are you in for it, Ron?"

"Nah. The rules say it's got to be a present member of the Cabinet. It's a stitch-up."

He is a man in whom hope is never extinguished and I think he might just have believed that.

2. Rhodri Tidies His Sock Drawer

It's a game even some professional historians like to play from time to time: counterfactuals. What if a single but apparently crucial incident in the past had not happened at all, or had happened differently? Suppose, for example, that on October 26, 1998, Ron Davies had arrived for his walk on Clapham Common five minutes later than he did. He would probably not have met the man who offered to take him for a drink and a meal and who then robbed him at knifepoint, an event which led to his resignation. If he had been delayed for only a few minutes, the next day he would have gone to his office as usual as Secretary of State for Wales. Then Labour would have been spared the indignities and opprobrium generated by the second Welsh leadership contest. As a result of that, the party might have done rather better in the elections the following May. If so then, as First Secretary, Ron might well have presided over the assembly with all the authority of a majority administration. Labour would be running the show as Labour was used to running the show in large parts of Wales. They could have talked all day about inclusivity but they wouldn't have had to mean it.

Then again: if Rhodri Morgan hadn't made a casual joke at Tony Blair's expense in the Tea Room of the House of Commons, would the tumult which was to characterise Welsh politics for sixteen months from October 1998 ever have taken place?

Or to go back even further. What if Lady Megan Lloyd-George had realised she was too gravely ill to fight the general election of March 1966 and had withdrawn? Would Welsh political life have taken an entirely different course over the following thirty years or so?

Lady Megan's career traces some of the most important developments in Welsh politics, particularly in rural Wales, during a large part of the twentieth century. The youngest child of the Liberal Prime Minister, David Lloyd George, she won Anglesey for the Liberals in 1929. She was the first woman to be elected in Wales and it was more than twenty years before two more women won seats, one of whom served only briefly. It wasn't until 1974 that Wales took the plunge for a fourth time, when Ann Clwyd won Aberdare in a by-election. This record suggests that the attitude of political parties in Wales towards women, in particular Labour, might have contributed to the bitter rows over selection procedures which, as we'll come to later, emerged during the selection process for the first assembly elections.

Lady Megan's career also reflected the way in which party politics in Wales went through perhaps its most significant change in the twentieth century: the decline of the Liberal Party and the rise of Labour. Many of the people who then won seats in rural Wales were similar in temperament to the old Liberals, cautiously radical, Welsh-speaking Nonconformists in the main. But they were also political realists and had joined the Labour Party. In 1951 Lady Megan lost her seat to one of them, Cledwyn Hughes, who in the sixties became Secretary of State for Wales and later Minister of Agriculture.

Lady Megan got the message. In 1957 she fought a by-election in Carmarthen for Labour and defeated the Liberal candidate. It was a longer physical journey than it was a political one, perhaps. The changes she made in her approach were in tune with the times, and there was little criticism involved in the enlightened self-interest in her moving from one party to another, especially as the Liberals, even in rural Wales, seemed to be on the verge of extinction. In these new circumstances Carmarthen was a perfectly safe seat for Lady Megan.

However, as the election of March 1966 approached, she became increasingly ill. Encouraging messages were sent to the constituency from London, where she was undergoing treatment, but her cancer was so advanced that she was unable to visit the constituency at all, although her biographer, Mervyn Jones, believes she didn't know she was dying.

The Pontypridd lawyer, Gwilym Prys-Davies, (now Lord Prys-Davies) did all the necessary political work on her behalf to such good effect that Lady Megan got a record majority of more than nine thousand. If Prys-Davies had been the candidate himself it's difficult to believe he wouldn't have won. After all, the government had been clinging on by its fingernails since

October 1964: there was a mood in the country to give them a proper mandate and the voters duly delivered a Labour majority of 97.

But only a few months later, on July 14, Lady Megan was dead and Gwynfor Evans, the Plaid Cymru president, had been elected in her place. The luckless Prys-Davies was second in the by-election. There were plenty of explanations for the shift, not least the kind of economic crisis which in one form or another haunted Labour from the moment it took office in 1964. There was yet another run on sterling; the bank rate had been raised that day and the Prime Minister, Harold Wilson, made a statement in the Commons which foreshadowed the stringent economic measures, including a pay freeze, which were to be taken the following week. Given that Labour had a majority of almost a hundred, no doubt the people of Carmarthen felt particularly free to make their comments on this performance in the only way open to them.

Gwynfor Evans's arrival in Westminster as the first Plaid Cymru Member of Parliament gave his party new public credibility and at the same time created a home for the votes of people who wanted to thumb their noses at Labour's performance, particularly in places like the South Wales valleys where a relentless pit closure programme was under way: 34,000 mining jobs, getting on for half the total, were lost in the years between 1964 and 1970. In Rhondda West in 1967 and Caerphilly in 1968, Plaid Cymru gave the proprietorial Labour Party an unprecedented scare, twice coming within a few percentage points of fresh by-election victories. The constitutional question was opened and the consequences led in a direct line to the creation of the Welsh assembly.

So you wonder if Lady Megan's doctors had given her different advice, or if her illness had taken a more rapid course and there had consequently been no by-election, would an elected Welsh assembly now be going about its business in Cardiff Bay? I think the answer has to be yes, that similar trends would eventually have revealed themselves in a different way but, such is the appeal of virtual history, we can never be sure.

In the same way the incident between Rhodri Morgan and Tony Blair in the Commons Tea Room seems trivial but it might just have been the key to many of the unexpected events that were to follow in Wales. Given the mysteries that persist in this area it still seems to be as good an explanation as any other.

The most curious thing about this whole affair of the Welsh Labour leadership and the consequences that flowed from it is why, in May 1997, Rhodri Morgan was unexpectedly excluded from ministerial office. He'd served on the front bench as a spokesman on Wales throughout the previous five years in opposition and there was absolutely no hint that he would not take his place in Government after the election. Well, perhaps there was a hint, but only a demented conspiracy theorist would have spotted it at the time.

It came, or so it is now interpreted, at Welsh Night at the Labour conference in October 1996. Welsh Night is an event of stupendous sentimentality, full of MPs singing and other unimaginably awful events. By tradition the Leader always comes along and makes a little speech of praise and encouragement. (The tone of the whole affair can be judged by the occasion on which Harold Wilson apologised for the absence of his wife, Mary, who, he said, was unfortunately in bed with a cold. Immediately a bunch of politicians and trade unionists who had never heard of diplomatic illness, or diplomatic anything come to that, formed an impromptu choir and marched off to her bedroom to give her a few verses of *Cwm Rhondda* at full blast. I believe events of this kind explain her determination to get Harold out of politics as soon as possible.) On that evening in 1996, Tony Blair naturally told everyone what a brilliant team he had looking after Welsh matters. Ron Davies, Win Griffiths, the MP for Bridgend, and Rhodri. Then, according to Rhodri, he made a rather curious remark.

"He said what a wonderful future I had in front of me."

Well, who wouldn't blush to hear that from the man you believe is shortly to become prime minister? Rhodri felt (and who wouldn't?) that it must be the political equivalent of a Masonic handshake.

"You took it to mean that you were guaranteed a junior ministerial role in the Welsh Office but that he might be thinking of giving you something much sexier and more glamorous. The Foreign Office or something."

This is not an unreasonable point of view, even in a trade where the meaning of ordinary words is proverbially elusive. But the old hands at reading signs and omens thought otherwise, particularly, as is the way of soothsayers, after the event.

"Subsequently," Rhodri said, "people have said that was him trying to say you've been written out of the script. It was a curious remark to make. Most of them read it very positively. In fact it was the reverse. He meant a brilliant career on the outside. On the back benches or a select committee or something."

Events have shown that that was exactly what Tony Blair meant, or came to mean. If that's the case it was a very cruel piece of sarcasm, unworthy of a leader of the Opposition and in contradiction of Tony Blair's carefully cultivated reputation for being 'a good guy'. This also provides further support for the view that politicians are not as other people. They speak a language which is English and isn't English at one and the same time; and although many of them are outwardly mature, well-educated, experienced and willing at the drop of a hat to tell other people what to do, they are also a jangling mass of nerves, inadequacy and self-doubt. They are, in many ways, not grown-up. Despite this, though the central puzzle remains. Why wasn't Rhodri given a job?

We have to remember here that he wasn't refused something in the Cabinet. He hadn't been expecting to be Home Secretary or Minister of Agriculture. His sights were set no higher than parliamentary under-secretary of state at the Welsh Office, pretty well the lowest form of ministerial life there is. In the evolutionary chain of politics if the prime minister is *homo sapiens*, a junior minister at the Welsh Office is an amoeba.

Anyway, his assumption and everyone else's was that the whole thing was in the bag. Why not, after all? So on Saturday, May 3, he sat by the phone and waited for the call from Downing Street. Nothing. His colleague Win Griffiths was in the same position and they rang each other at regular intervals. Then there was a curious incident. It was announced that Peter Hain had been given a job in the Welsh Office. No-one had expected it, but both Rhodri and Win then assumed that, like Scotland, Wales was to get an extra minister, making four in all.

"Then I had a phone call of some description from Ron. I can't quite remember now. All I can remember is I was desperately trying to occupy my time. I actually tidied my sock drawer for the first time in my life. I spent hours and hours folding them all neatly."

Saturday passed somehow.

On Sunday there were more phone calls from Ron, discouraging ones, saying it wasn't going well. Then it was Downing Street on the line.

"Tony Blair comes on and says he's sorry but he hasn't got a place for me in the administration. I said, 'Why's that, Tony?' He mentioned age. I think he was pretty well at the end of his tether then, but even so I think it was pretty insulting what he said. I don't think he realised. He thought he was being nice. But he was implying, (a) you're too old; (b) you haven't got the ability. It's not a very nice thing to say."

If Rhodri Morgan has made a reputation for one thing in particular it is his unwillingness, or perhaps his inability, to refrain from saying what he thinks. It is an engaging trait, although a dangerous one, and he wasn't going to hold back when Blair went on to make a remarkable comment.

"He said: 'When I make my appointments to junior ministries I make them on the basis that anybody who comes in, even as a parliamentary under-secretary, must be capable of proceeding to full Cabinet.'"

It was a preposterous statement even from a very tired man and Rhodri told him so. "I said: 'Tony, you're not being serious. I know that a good half of them aren't capable of entering your Cabinet.'"

In this context the name Tony Banks springs to mind. Banks, who pronounced himself "gobsmacked" to be made Minister of Sport at that time, is clever and funny, but as far as discretion and reticence is concerned he makes Rhodri look like a mime artist. He lasted longer than anyone might have expected as a minister but voluntarily slipped away from government after a couple of years to run England's (eventually failed) bid to stage the football World Cup in 2006. Nor, in fairness, could it have been said of Win Griffiths, the mild and conscientious MP, who did get a junior job in the Welsh Office but who was sacked a year or so later. Even less did it apply to Win's successor, Jon Owen Jones.

As Rhodri explained what happened, I got a sense that Blair, despite the preoccupations of the time, had strong feelings of guilt over his behaviour. Most of the members of what Rhodri calls the "dispossessed", the people who had failed to make it from Shadow jobs into the real thing, didn't hear personally from the Prime Minister at all. But the following week Rhodri was asked to go to Downing Street where he once again spoke his mind.

"I did have a bit of a go at him. I said: 'Look, Tony, when you spoke to me and you referred to age and suchlike I didn't know that you'd appointed Glenda Jackson. Now, Glenda's sixty-one and I'm fifty-seven. You knew that by the time I open my *Guardian* the next morning I'm going to see that Glenda's been appointed and she's four years older than me. So what's all this bullshit about me being too old, because if I'm too old at fifty-seven and you've appointed Glenda who's sixty-one.

"Now you know that when you tell me, even though I don't but you know I was going to find out the following morning when I opened the *Guardian* and I saw the full list.'

"Tony says: 'Ah, but I wouldn't have appointed Glenda chairman of a select committee.'"

"Bullshit," Rhodri shouted almost three years later as he recalled the incident. "Who wants to be chairman of a select committee if they can be a junior minister? They are not comparable jobs. Anyway, it wasn't him who made me chairman of a select committee; it was Nick Brown, the Chief Whip. He rang me and said, 'Rhodri, I feel really bad about what's happened. You can have any select committee you want, provided I haven't promised it to someone else.'

"It was nothing to do with Tony Blair."

It would be understandable if the object of this kind of treatment, particularly because of the sense that something was being concealed, felt a continuing resentment and a serious desire for revenge, to get one back on Blair. Rhodri has consistently maintained it wasn't the case. That's what he says and we must take his word for it. Nevertheless, it reveals a saintly forbearance, which most people had not previously detected, and his language and his manner sit uneasily alongside this disclaimer. He says his wife, Julie, who'd just become an MP herself in May 1997, was fumingly angry and couldn't understand why he wasn't resentful.

It's also the case that his account of these conversations suggests very strongly that Blair had a sense of unease about the way he'd treated him. At the same time it's possible to get a flavour of Rhodri's style, in which tact doesn't figure very prominently, and which was almost certainly a factor in his being refused the job in the first place. In itself, though, it doesn't seem enough to explain Blair's decision to exclude him. And that mystery remains. No-one I've spoken to, at all levels of the Labour Party, can come up with any convincing reason for the Prime Minister's attitude.

Most people fall back on that familiar political phrase: Rhodri is his own worst enemy. His wild and woolly appearance, a tall, well-built man with Brillo pad hair, a shambolic manner and an individualistic dress sense which at times suggested a hurried visit to a charity shop, was certainly one factor which marked him out as a dubious character for a government which has made a religion of image. In the light of this it was interesting that, as these events unfolded, Rhodri became noticeably better groomed, if not exactly a clothes horse.

He's an attractive phrasemaker, uncomfortably so sometimes, sharp and ironic. "Does a one-legged duck swim in circles?" his reply to Jeremy Paxman when asked if he was standing for the Welsh Labour leadership, has been quoted with admiration ever since. When, at one stage, Ron Davies failed to announce as expected a definite site for the assembly building, Rhodri said that to call it a dog's dinner would be an insult to the pet food industry. (His own early intervention as First Secretary to postpone the scheme for yet another examination perhaps puts that wounding comment in a rather different light.) "Winners don't whinge," he said to me once (or was it whingers don't win?). "I wasn't a shirt-warmer for Ron Davies and I'm not one for Alun Michael." He's so good at this sort of thing, he communicates with the public so arrestingly, it comes as a surprise to realise that he's often an unimpressive speechmaker who can lead himself quite easily into incoherence as he bubbles away like one of those hot springs in New Zealand.

In some ways, although not in that one, he reminds me of Austin Mitchell, another great Labour eccentric, whose chaotic appearance and speed of tongue haven't helped his ambitions for political advancement. In conversation one evening Michael White, the Political Editor of the *Guardian*, said: "The trouble with you, Austin, is you're clever, pluralist and funny. The Labour Party will put up with two of those things, but not all three."

You could say the same sort of thing about Rhodri, and although he doesn't have anything like the same intellectual weight, he's not off message in big matters in the way Austin is over Europe in particular. Sometimes, indeed, it's quite difficult to establish what Rhodri's message actually is.

But his exclusion remains a puzzle. Minor matters are sometimes mentioned, in particular his continued opposition to the building of a barrage in Cardiff Bay, a project which, even after it had been completed, he was still unable to endorse other than grudgingly. Like a lot of people he had perfectly good reasons for opposing it, but a man who can resent a piece of civil engineering for thirteen years perhaps might not be quite flexible enough to meet the demands of government, particularly in the Welsh Office which had to point to this development as one of the achievements demonstrating the sparkling new image of a thoroughly modernised Wales. Rhodri is the second obsessive figure to appear in this story, but by no means the last one.

One Labour official certainly thought his attitude to Cardiff Bay might have been of particular significance. "When Blair is trying to show what a wonderfully new Labour pro-businessman kind of person he is, he comes down to the Bay and says what a brilliant project it is and Rhodri is standing behind him telling the press what a load of junk it is."

These things mount up and, searching for an explanation, Rhodri lights on a brief moment of tension between himself and Blair, what he calls a little spat.

"I'd had an extremely close relationship with Tony Blair. I'd worked with him for two years. Almost lived in his pocket when he first got into the Shadow Cabinet in 1988. He never used to eat in the Commons in the evenings. He always used to go home to see the kids. I used to admire this.

"I remember one evening, perhaps in 95 or 96, I wandered into the Tea Room to get a light supper. There was Tony Blair in the queue in front of me. So I said, jokingly, 'Hey, Tony, giving up the habits of a lifetime. You're not the good family man any more. You're having dinner here instead of going home to the kids.'

"And he turned to me and he showed his teeth. 'I am still the good family man.' Oh, God, I thought, I've said the wrong thing here.

"What I didn't realise was that the story was about to break about him sending his son Euan to the Oratory School.* He might have thought I already knew and that I thought he was, as it were, putting the family before the cause of socialism pure and simple. That I was putting the knife in. That's the only time I've seen him glare at me or look really quite hostile."

People who don't spend a great deal of their time mixing with politicians and considering the nuances of political life, might ask whether it's possible that something so trivial could influence a man who, after all, was Leader of the Opposition and would, by definition, have more important things to think about. The answer is yes.

In this story you can see clearly Rhodri's irrepressible capacity for getting up people's noses, something he doesn't always fully appreciate himself. But you can also see in subsequent events the significance of personality in politics (which is often played down by the theorists) as well as the detailed interest a Prime Minister must and does take in who is going to fill even

* The argument over Blair sending Euan to the London Oratory provoked one of those old socialist theological arguments still enjoyed by New Labour. Although it was a Catholic school within the state system, it had opted out of local authority control and interviewed children for places, officially to examine their religious suitability. Blair was accused of being hypocritical for sending his (Catholic) son there. The theory behind the criticism is that if the children of senior politicians have a bad time in useless schools then there'll be that much more incentive for governments to improve the education system as a whole. It re-emerged in a slightly different form in the spring of 2000 when ministers, led by the Chancellor, Gordon Brown, attacked what they said were the elitist selection procedures of Oxbridge colleges.

the most negligible posts in his administration. It is part of the machinery of control which is at least as important to a government as is the broad sweep of policy. At the same time it's comforting to reflect that events in Wales have demonstrated that, as you struggle to subdue one ferret, another pops its head out of the sack.

The immediate effect of Rhodri's exclusion was to make him the object of rare political sympathy, the victim of an injustice. A week or so after the general election he went to speak at a big Labour dinner in the Rhondda. As he and other leading figures in the Welsh party went into the hall, five hundred people stood to applaud. He thought it was a mark of respect and congratulations to them all, but one of his companions said, "No, that's for you".

The sympathetic ovation seems to have given him an idea. He thought to himself: "They think you're good enough, even if the Prime Minister doesn't." Long before May 1997 even, he'd announced publicly that, if and when a Welsh assembly was set up, he would want to serve there rather than Westminster. There was no reason now why he shouldn't try to become its leader. At the end of the party's UK conference in October that year he said he'd stand. For those who like irony, he was encouraged in this by Welsh delegates from the Transport & General Workers Union, the organisation which was to be instrumental in denying him the job the second time round.

It seems pretty clear that if Rhodri had been a junior minister at the Welsh Office there would have been substantial obstacles in the way of his standing. A backbencher, particularly a disappointed backbencher, didn't need anyone's permission to take part in another democratic contest. If he'd been a ministerial colleague, though, it's difficult to see how he could have avoided discussing it with Ron and almost inevitably becoming part of some overall Labour strategy.

Rhodri is ambiguous about this. He says a job might have made a difference. He says it might have made a difference, too, if Ron had indicated during the referendum campaign that he was interested in the leadership.

"I don't know whether I would have changed my mind. I might have. In no way was I occupying space that was already occupied. There was a seven-month gap between Donald Dewar [the Scottish Secretary] saying he was going to run for First Minister in Scotland and Ron saying he was going to run."

Did he ask Ron?

"Not directly. It's not my job to."

Rhodri is a politician and so, by definition these days, fiercely ambitious. His manner, his appearance, mask this, as they do in the public mind the fact that he was educated at Oxford and Harvard and was born into the very heart of the Welsh cultural and academic establishment. His father, T.J. Morgan, an academic and writer, was one of the leading scholars of the deepest intricacies of the Welsh language. The characteristics which make people warm to Rhodri as a person who is somehow more 'real' that many others in public life can also lead opponents to underestimate him. Like Ken Livingstone, although without Livingstone's agenda, he appeals to the kind of constituency which doesn't like regulation politicians. There is about both men a kind of wounded innocence calculated to appeal to the sentimental streak in many voters.

Well, the theory runs, if Rhodri had got a job in the first place we wouldn't have been in this difficulty now. That's because some virtual historians go on to say that it was the exhausting nature of the contest against Rhodri that led Ron into a state of emotional and psychological weakness. Having won, he did what other kinds of fighters do: he dropped his guard. His walk on Clapham Common and the consequences of it were the direct result of the pounding he had taken as he slugged it out with Rhodri up and down Wales throughout that summer. That, at least, is one version put forward by people who know Ron well.

Maybe. But there were serious repercussions for Rhodri, too. When Ron resigned as the leader of the Welsh Labour Party on October 29, 1998, Downing Street was faced with an unwelcome problem. What kind of credible figure could they get to replace him? What about Rhodri? The discussion was brief. No. He was not acceptable. In that case there was only one serious contender: the man who had so abruptly succeeded Ron as Welsh Secretary, Alun Michael. It was from this point on, I think, that people began to realise how much flannel there was in Labour's awesome reputation for all-seeing mastery of the political machine. It turned out that there were plenty of things they couldn't fix, certainly lots of things they couldn't fix discreetly, although we weren't to know at this stage quite how unfixable Wales would eventually prove to be.

There was an indication soon enough. For a moment Downing Street and Alun Michael conjured up the hope that something described as 'a dream team' could be cobbled together. Alun would get a free run and be elected Welsh Labour leader. Rhodri would join him on the ticket, as would Wayne David, the former leader of the Labour MPs in the European Parliament. Wayne, who'd announced he was resigning as an MEP in favour of the assembly, was to discover a few months later that he'd actually organised himself a one-way ticket to the job centre.* In the meantime Rhodri's response to the proposal was characteristic.

"The answer is very simple. It comes in folding ballot papers. It goes right back to ancient Greece and it's called democracy and it has reached Wales, but perhaps only in patches."

He was to find out a little later that the party leadership's definition of democracy was not the same as his. He wanted to explain that he hadn't run against Ron out of some act of defiance, as an act of resentment for not having been given a ministerial job. He got a chilly reception. That was exactly what they did think and he was told: "Well, you did run against a government minister."

Nor can he have improved his chances, such is his unerring ability to make matters worse, by hauling the Prime Minister's official spokesman, Alastair Campbell, before the Commons' Public Administration Select Committee, of which he was chairman. It was presented in the media as Rhodri, the people's champion, shining the light of open government into the dark corners where spin doctors plan to deceive the public. It is rarely a good idea to antagonise perhaps the most influential non-elected person in British politics.

Despite all that, though, you now realise that, as far as New

---

*Wayne's bad luck ended unexpectedly the following year when he was selected as Labour's Westminster candidate in Caerphilly in succession to Ron who had decided to remain with the assembly.

Labour are concerned, the rules of politics are such that standing for election in an open contest can be interpreted as a shocking act of disloyalty. This is still the case even if you have some reason to believe one aspect of your career has been unreasonably thwarted and you now wish to test the opinions of a different electorate. More than that, you are not told what the rules are, so you can never be sure when you will be accused of some offence. It is a way of going on that would have been much admired by the late Joe Stalin.

At the same time, anyone who remembers Labour in the early eighties, when most people did exactly what they felt like and so brought the party to the brink of ruin, will realise why the new regime laid such an emphasis on discipline, on the grim virtues of conformity. The cheering thing, as people were to discover in Wales, is that the party machine is as imperfect as the rest of us and it can't make the system work. In Downing Street all the experts and advisers with an answer for every occasion were entirely unaware that they were actually engaged in demonstrating to the British public in general, and Welsh voters in particular, that they were not as smart as they thought they were.

3: George Lends a Hand

If it's possible to imagine Alun Michael doing anything as frivolous as whistling, and so wasting a few precious seconds he might otherwise have been devoting to the minutiae of government, then you'd guess that the morning of October 27, 1998 might have provided that rare, carefree moment. He was Deputy Home Secretary, a role that gave him endless scope for working day and night on all those social problems which, as he'd tell you if you asked, and even if you didn't, had long been one of his main areas of concern. He was a pal of the Prime Minister's and was assured of his patronage, something publicly underwritten that day by his promotion to the Privy Council. It was a pat on the back to show he was doing well, not a new job but surely an indication that a new and better job couldn't be long delayed. He was now the Right Honourable Alun Michael MP, unobtrusively moving up a step on the political ladder. He rang his mother in North Wales to tell her the news, then went off to lunch with a journalist from the *Financial Times*.

He had just finished the first course when his pager went. He was needed immediately at No.10. He borrowed the journalist's mobile phone and called Downing Street. They wouldn't tell him what it was about. Just get here fast. The good times were about to come to an abrupt end. That promotion had come faster than anyone could have anticipated. Ron had resigned and by mid-afternoon Alun was in the Cabinet as Welsh Secretary. But there was another vital decision that would have to be taken soon. Should he now try to become the leader of the Labour Party in Wales and, as such, first secretary-designate of the national assembly.

Throughout the sixteen months of controversy that were to follow, Alun was portrayed by his critics as a man who had little interest in being a Welsh politician, a man who at best had been indifferent to devolution on its first outing twenty years before, who contemplated being Welsh Labour leader only because he was acting under the detailed instructions of the Prime Minister. Alun's own account was almost exactly the opposite.

When I interviewed him on the day he announced he would be a candidate he said that the decision had been entirely his. It was clear that it was his duty to take on the job and he had gone to Tony Blair to tell him so. If anything, he implied, he was telling the leadership how it was going to be. When I talked to him more than a year later, though, it emerged that events hadn't been quite that straightforward. But he maintained that the initiative had come from him.

"I went to Tony and said I've looked at the situation and this is going to be a big challenge. The implementation of the assembly has got to be done properly. It's got to be effective. I think this involves me standing for the leadership of the assembly."

"What did he say?"

"That was his view."

"Just like that?"

"There was certainly quite a bit of discussion about the immediate challenges. I did test the decision out with a variety of people. I talked to my family. I talked to a variety of people involved with Welsh politics and in the Labour Party."

"In a government famous for its meticulous political control," I suggested, "you'd expect them to examine the options. They might have asked Rhodri in for a chat, for instance."

"There was a period when those sort of things were happening. Rhodri was one of the people I talked to."

At Downing Street's request, senior Welsh Labour figures had in fact urgently examined other possibilities. At a sensitive time in the Irish peace process (where it is practically always a sensitive time) Paul Murphy, the MP for Torfaen, couldn't be spared from his job as Minister of State at the Northern Ireland Office. Someone suggested Peter Hain, much admired by the Prime Minister as a house-trained left-winger: he was too junior and, in difficult circumstances, not Welsh enough. That's to say, not Welsh at all. Someone else said presciently that Rhodri was bound to get his hands on the levers of power one day, why not give him a go now? Unthinkable. It had to be Alun.

There was one other consideration that emerged. The view now was that the two jobs had to be yoked together, the Secretary of State moving on oiled wheels into the office of First Secretary of the National Assembly for Wales. It wasn't just not wanting Rhodri, it would henceforth be argued. The administrative and constitutional imperatives demanded that Alun should get the job. It was the first time most of us had heard this argument but it meant the Government was in effect saying there should be no contest of any kind.

In all this Alun has been relentlessly, and perhaps unjustly, criticised. Like most people I believed his real political ambitions didn't lie in Wales, but elsewhere. But what was also evident was that he had a highly-developed sense of duty and loyalty and, once it was clear that he had to bite the Welsh bullet, he turned his formidable capacity for hard work and attention to detail to his new task. These admirable qualities were his greatest strength but, in the rough way of politics, they were also instrumental in his downfall. In this story Alun Michael is obsessive number three.

Like many extremely conscientious people he often seems incapable of distinguishing between what is important and what is not. Thus, when people accused him, as they frequently did, of not having been a supporter of devolution in the seventies he wasn't content simply to deny it, provide a little evidence in support of his case, and leave it at that. Instead he became a one-tune jukebox. He could not mention the word devolution without adding a kind of footnote: "...which as you know I supported during the sixties and the seventies".

Even when I talked to him as late as January 2000 he felt it necessary to explain it all over again to me, who didn't care much either way and who had no say in his future. "If we'd won the referendum in 1979 I would never have stood for Parliament. I would have stood for the assembly perhaps if I'd had the opportunity. I thought devolution was dead for my lifetime. I thought it would come back eventually but I didn't expect it to come back as early as it did...." Well, we mustn't tread on territory that properly belongs to the manufacturers of powerful sedatives, but you get the gist of it. The truth is that if they'd given out medals for the 1979 devolution campaign, Alun would have clanked around in his every day, like Private Jones in *Dad's Army*. Like Rhodri Morgan, whose mortal enemy he was over the Cardiff Bay barrage, he finds it difficult to move on. And, of course, the more he said it, the more people were inclined to believe it wasn't true.

This relentless, grinding aspect of Alun's character means that he is not a man of immediate popular appeal. He has admirers and loyal supporters within the party, particularly his constituency party, because they have come to value the very qualities that are such a liability when it comes to a personality contest. On *Newsnight* he was described as a man who "...is not a household name, even in his own household". Small and lean and fair-haired, grey-suited, with business-like spectacles, he has the appearance and manner of a harassed junior science master in a failing comprehensive. He is earnest and thorough and reliable and so, the argument went, the very man to be told by Tony Blair what to do and the very man to do exactly as he was told. Sceptics said that, just as Ron had 'sorry' written on his hand when he gave his first post-Clapham Common interviews, so Alun had 'Wales' written on his, to remind him of what he was supposed to be doing.

He doesn't in any way accept this version, but that's irrelevant. In politics what people believe to be true is usually decisive. He was now in a contest which in the public mind was between brilliant, wronged Rhodri who wanted nothing more than to serve the Welsh people, and boring yes-man Alun who looked as though he'd been pushed through the door into the Coliseum without even the time to pick up his net and his trident. In these circumstances even the weight of his backing by the party hierarchy would probably not be enough to guarantee victory. In some ways, indeed, quite the reverse.

Peter Hain had been put into the Welsh Office specifically because of his campaigning skills and he'd been a leading figure in one narrow victory – in the referendum of September 1997. He became Alun's campaign manager and he thought this one looked even more difficult.

"It was a huge risk. The stakes were extremely high. The consequences for the party generally of Alun losing in Wales would have been very serious. In early November it seemed like mission impossible. Some of my friends said I'd accepted the job too quickly. Virtually all of the parliamentary party thought Rhodri would win."

That outcome – defeat for Alun Michael – would inevitably

be portrayed as defeat for Tony Blair, and not without reason. This was no time for being squeamish.

There were two main strategies employed on Alun's behalf. The first was to make it a long campaign – the beginning of November to the end of February – to allow time for the circumstances of Alun's candidacy to be airbrushed out of the picture as thoroughly as possible. It would also mean that, as Secretary of State, he could get lots of publicity by going round week after week announcing important-sounding things, particularly any bits of good news. He would come to seem like the man who should naturally continue to be in charge. The second, which in many people's minds came to represent a disreputable revival of Old Labour power-broking, was to have the contest decided by an electoral college.

Although the term electoral college has a reassuringly respectable ring to it, in the form it was used by Labour in the Welsh leadership election and again (providing striking evidence that even the most sophisticated people don't learn from experience) in the selection process for the London Mayor, it remained the weapon of choice of the stitch-up tendency in its ceaseless quest for methods of stifling dissent. Even so, despite its naked intentions, the nothing-up-my-sleeve party operators who introduced it were fond of saying: "The electoral college was good enough to elect Tony Blair and John Prescott so it's good enough for Wales."

Rhodri Morgan's retort was: "If they're trying to tell you that, they're selling you snake oil", an accurate description of the process since, in the Blair-Prescott election, the trades unions balloted their members while in the Welsh contest there was no obligation on them to do so. Whatever the legal niceties involved, and there are those who say the party has no authority to insist on specific methods by which unions should consult their members in this process, it was a political and public relations disaster. Whatever people said about drawing lines in the sand, putting things behind them, going forward in a spirit of unity and all the other weasel words that come so easily at times like this, the election did not settle the question. Instead the method used made certain it remained open.

After a campaign fought with superficial tolerance and understanding between one side and the other, an attitude which barely concealed the activities of the usual dirty tricks departments, the result was announced at the St. David's Hotel in Cardiff Bay on the morning of Saturday, February 20, 1999. As expected, Alun won fairly easily in the section for MPs, MEPs and assembly candidates – 58 per cent to Rhodri's 42 per cent. As expected, too, Rhodri had an almost two-to-one majority among the individual party members – the popular vote. In the end it was the unions – the unpopular vote – who were decisive, almost 64 per cent for Alun.

When it comes to the principle of OMOV – one member one vote – there are any number of machine politicians who think the word democratic is used in the same sense in the Labour Party as it was in the title of the old German Democratic Republic, to the outside world essentially a piece of gallows humour. They talk interminably about the origins and traditions of the party being represented in the tripartite nature of the electoral college and about many other things which are entirely foreign to people who lead normal lives. But even then it's not necessarily the college itself people object to, but failure to apply the principle of OMOV within it. Yet it was a principle which had only fairly recently been shoved into the party's constitution in the teeth of opposition from the vested interests who had run it for so long. It was perhaps the single most significant break with a past in which trade union leaders had often acted like a politburo, but without its Soviet counterpart's innate sense of fair play.

Every indication was that, if each union had balloted its members, Rhodri would have won the election. But there we were, New Labour, old fix. Or that's what it looked like, and there were by now a lot of people who thought the party's behaviour should match its rhetoric a little more closely. Alun's victory was another of those events which actually contained some of the seeds of his eventual defeat. Perhaps he should have had a premonition of that, not least because of the company he was keeping.

The man who most clearly represented the persistence of the old, and the man subjected to the most fierce denunciations from Rhodri's supporters, was George Wright, the Welsh regional secretary of the Transport & General Workers Union. In the early seventies George had been a protégé of the then T&G general secretary, Jack Jones, a man who could have given Chairman Mao a few lessons in keeping his hands on the levers of power. George had been sent to Wales from the Midlands as a step up the ladder of the union hierarchy but, for various reasons, had got stuck. He was an important figure in establishing the Wales TUC (he was its first general secretary, thanks to the munificence of the T&G, whose money was instrumental in getting the organisation established at all) and a substantial and successful figure in Welsh public life. By the time the Welsh leadership election came round he was within a few months of retirement. A number of the unions avoided anything that looked much like OMOV. The AEEU (engineers and electricians), for example, held a delegate meeting at which it was decided that its 65,000 votes should go to Alun, but among Rhodri's supporters George Wright was picked out as the chief villain. He had sixty thousand members and, he said, the union could not afford to ballot them. A decision was taken privately to cast the votes for Alun.

Even in these circumstances George wasn't particularly embarrassed by accusations of his behaving like an old-fashioned union boss (the trade union 'barons' as the newspapers like to call them). More than that, he seemed to relish the public recognition that he was a man who could get things done. At a dinner not much more than a week before the election result was declared, he told me: "If the party want me to fix it, I fix it. If they wanted me to fix it for Patrick Hannan, I'd do it."

Maybe, but if I wanted something fixed I'd probably stay away from George Wright. Although he's able, energetic and shrewd, he's also proverbially unlucky. He'd been a leading figure in the campaign for a 'No' vote in the 1975 European referendum. His side lost. He was one of the chief organisers for a 'Yes' vote in the 1979 devolution referendum. The majority against him was four to one. He failed on two separate occasions to be elected general secretary of the T&G. Perhaps it would have paid Alun Michael to be more superstitious. You might run, but you can't hide from the curse of George Wright and, even stripping away the supernatural, it's obvious that

George's part in the election added to the resentment which was to be so decisive over the next year.

Indeed, even as people were milling around the St. David's Hotel on the morning of February 20, assuring each other that the acrimony of the campaign was now behind them, the resentment was simmering away as usual. Rhodri's team began asking how it was that Alun's supporters apparently knew the margin of victory on the previous day, despite the fact that it was a secret ballot. It was just one of their continuing doubts about the whole process. It looked as if someone was up to something but then, this being the Labour Party, someone nearly always was.

Eager as always to try and block another hole in the disciplinary colander, the following month the party's national executive committee announced that it would henceforth be against the rules to criticise publicly the conduct of any internal party election, an exercise in futility which reminded many people that New Labour hadn't entirely broken with the traditions it claimed to have dismantled.

Much later, but before the events that were to make him First Secretary, I asked Rhodri if he'd thought at the time he could beat Alun Michael.

"Oh, yes. Yes, certainly."

"Do you think you were swizzed out of it?"

"It's what you call genetically modified democracy."

It was over but it wasn't over. After the result had been declared Rhodri told the *Daily Telegraph*: "I have to hold myself in reserve in case Alun doesn't get elected on May 6."

And, as we know, at the same time Ron Davies was thinking the same thought.

Alun did get elected, of course, but in a story shot through with paradox, that might well have been due in substantial part to the acrimony generated by the second leadership contest. In so far as it's possible to tell, it was probably the single most important factor in costing Labour an overall majority in the assembly elections, but if the party had had a majority Alun would in all probability not have been one its members, thanks to the way in which the additional member system works.

Peter Hain, who'd brought Alun through it all, was now launched on his third campaign in two years – this time for the assembly elections themselves. He was acutely aware of the fact that his team's success had made this next job even more difficult.

"Anyone who denied that the leadership contest alienated a lot of Labour's traditional support would be an idiot. It did. There was a huge price paid for that election and for Alun Michael's victory, and I was part of being responsible for that price being paid."

Hain is an exotic figure in the mundane world of Welsh politics. In the Welsh Office he was known to civil servants as 'His Orangeness' because of his year-round tan, something that goes with his South African accent but which at the same time never looks absolutely right, as though the bulb in the sun lamp isn't quite strong enough. He's been famous in politics for as long as most of us can remember, particularly as an anti-apartheid campaigner but also, it's strange to recall now, as a leading Young Liberal. He's charming, intelligent, hard-working and ambitious with a good opinion of his own abilities. He's one of the few members of the government who can say the word socialist without laughing, which apparently provides him with a licence to give the party stern, old-fashioned lectures from time to time.

"Back in June or July of 1998 I gave a speech at an Institute of Welsh Affairs conference in Aberystwyth, and I said that Labour might not get an overall majority. It was prescient in some ways. I had no idea that Clapham Common would happen and that the bruising leadership contest would take place, but I always thought we were too complacent. The Labour Party in Wales had got used to winning for a generation and it felt it could just go on winning."

But the leadership election was only one element in a series of difficulties which Labour largely heaped on itself during that time. Another emerged from an impetus to 'do the right thing', always a dangerous instinct in politics and an unfamiliar idea in the Labour heartlands of industrial Wales. This was contained in a specific policy to produce an equal number of men and women candidates for the assembly elections. The mechanism chosen was that of 'twinning', a system whereby constituencies were formed into pairs which would, between them, nominate one man and one woman candidate.

It caused considerable resentment in some constituencies because it removed their traditional autonomy when it came to their most important form of patronage. It also diluted the idea of merit, whatever that might have consisted of when it came to choosing Labour candidates. Again, it is the case that, despite the number of formidable, not to say intimidating, women who have played leading roles in the Labour Party in Wales over the years, many men continue to resent the changed relationship between the sexes which has been one of the most conspicuous consequences of the decline of heavy industry. This was making that change official. It happened, even though some heads had to be banged together, but sullen acceptance was not the best mood for party workers who were expected to go out and maximise the vote at the election.

At the same time the Labour machine in London seemed to have some difficulty getting the hang of the principle of devolution. Wales has five constituencies in the European Parliament, all of which were won by Labour candidates in 1994. The proportional representation system introduced for the 1999 elections clearly meant that Labour could, at the very best, now hope to win three, probably only two of them. One of the MEPs, Wayne David, was off on his forlorn quest for an assembly seat, but the other four wanted to stand again.

When the Welsh list was announced by a central party committee, Glenys Kinnock and Eluned Morgan, sitting members, were put at numbers one and two. But at number three was someone called Lyndon Harrison, a man obscure even by the standards of the European Parliament, who had until then been a Cheshire member but who had been rejected by his own region. To call his inclusion insensitive is like describing Saddam Hussein as someone keen to get his own way. It upset the Welsh party, naturally, and it upset the Welsh voters who might not have known or cared who their MEPs were, but who were nevertheless under the impression that Labour were in the process of introducing a measure of self-determination for Wales and that this wasn't it.

Millbank, Labour's strategic headquarters, got the message rather late in the day. Eventually Harrison withdrew from the list because, it was said, of an injured foot. "There was nothing wrong with his foot the last time I saw him," an MP said afterwards, but it all worked out well for him in the end. In June, instead of losing in the European elections, as he would have done, Harrison featured in the Birthday Honours list and selflessly went to serve his country in the House of Lords.

At the same time, though, it's important to remember that the Labour Party in Wales doesn't need much help from outside when it comes to getting itself into a mess.

"Is it true," I asked Alun Michael, "that there was a feeling that some Labour local authorities were being run by incompetents and crooks?"

At times like this Alun falls back on speaking his native tongue which is, it seems, Esperanto.

"I wouldn't put it quite like that," he said. "There were those who voted against the established Labour hegemony in particular areas – sometimes for reasons of perception rather than reasons of reality."

Well, I don't know about the contest between perception and reality, but there were problems in local councils for which there was only too much solid evidence as far the voting public was concerned. On the same day as the assembly elections, Labour lost control of the Rhondda Cynon Taff Council to Plaid Cymru. Early the following month it was revealed that the council was, in effect, broke. It had lost at least £3 million on its direct labour organisation; it was supposed to have a reserve fund of £5 million but that was down to £650,000. It was embroiled in the Catch-22 of local government, being so hard up it couldn't afford to make people redundant in order to try to cut its losses.

Among its assets were 250 silk ties, 100 silk scarves and various cuff links and pens which had cost getting on for £6,000, as well as £2,000 worth of wines and spirits. The genius a trained Labour mind can bring to matters which would embarrass less talented people was then demonstrated by the explanation from one councillor that, since the price of drink was always put up in the Budget, buying ahead in large quantities, far from being an extravagance, was in fact an outstanding measure of frugality.

No-one said the Labour regime in Rhondda Cynon Taff had been dishonest, but in any case there was plenty of that to be going on with. The week after the elections Bernard Assinder, the former leader of Blaenau Gwent Council, was sentenced to 250 hours community service after an investigation into his expense claims. Shaun Stringer, who had stepped down as the leader of the Vale of Glamorgan Borough Council while the legal wheels turned, appeared in court at the end of the year and was ordered to repay £400 which he had spent on meals using his council credit card. Fourteen other charges were left on the file.

There were plenty of other investigations going on, and if the voters didn't know exactly what the misdemeanours were, they could smell them, not least because of long years of practice. By no means all the people who got into difficulties were Labour, but such incidents tend to revive memories of the not so distant days in many parts of Wales when the title councillor was considered to be synonymous with dishonesty and graft.

It's easy enough now, of course, to put these separate threads together and come to the conclusion that a kick in the teeth was Labour's inevitable fate on May 6, 1999, even if many of us didn't see it so clearly at the time. But the central question was, who was going to do the kicking? That it turned out to be Plaid Cymru was perhaps less surprising than the force with which the party administered the punishment.

As we gathered in the BBC's main current affairs radio studio at ten o'clock in the morning of May 7, Karl Davies, Plaid Cymru's chief executive, said he'd heard rumours that they'd won Rhondda. We didn't mention this on the air because Karl couldn't really believe it and went along with my calming interpretation that people tended to get a bit over-excited at that stage of an election. I was wrong, of course, as I would have been about Plaid Cymru winning Islwyn, Neil Kinnock's old parliamentary seat. Glenys Kinnock joined us for just long enough to say that Neil was "devastated."

Later Plaid Cymru were to win Llanelli, formerly as Labour as Keir Hardie's cloth cap, but that brought a separate, important consequence. The defeat meant it was more likely that Alun Michael would, after all, get a list seat in Mid and West Wales. For at least half the party that fact made the loss of Llanelli all the more painful. Even then, the calculations were still inconclusive, and remained so until the last result was declared. Rhodri Glyn Thomas of Plaid Cymru won Carmarthen East and Dinefwr. Defeat for Labour meant victory for Alun. At the last gasp he'd squeezed into the national assembly. It was perhaps yet another problem for him, despite the fairness the electoral system was supposed to provide. He was only in the assembly because the party he'd led had done badly. In other words he'd somehow been rewarded for failure, which was a further reason for some people to question the legitimacy of his position.

If that was a good reason for discomfort, so was the arithmetic. In a 60-member assembly Labour had won 28 seats and Plaid Cymru 17. The Conservatives, who could manage only a single first-past-the-post member, got nine seats and the Liberal Democrats six.

The campaign co-ordinator, Peter Hain, turned up in the studio to say he'd always warned the party against complacency and he put the poor performance down to disaffection with local authorities as well as incompetence and corruption. These were largely Labour local authorities, of course, but when things go wrong in local government the party leadership likes to imply that this is some mutant life form which, by an eerie coincidence, is called Labour as well, but actually has nothing to do with them.

In his untiring quest for someone else to blame, Hain was later to criticise the Labour Party as a whole, saying in an interview in the *New Statesman* the following month: "We have got ourselves into a dangerous situation where a Labour government appears as if it is being gratuitously offensive to its natural supporters."

His analysis went on: "The Government wants to give the impression that all its policies are targeted at Middle England - that relatively affluent part of the coalition Tony Blair brilliantly built up before the election. There seems to be an assumption that there is nowhere else for the core voters, Labour's natural supporters, to go. In fact there are several other options for that core support. For a start they can stay at home."

It's difficult to fault that analysis in the light of the 46 per cent turnout in the assembly election. Indifference to the whole devolution process was probably one factor, voter fatigue (stop asking us to make decisions all the time) another, a Labour government with a majority in Westminster of 179 a third. The 'It's only a Welsh election so it won't change our lives' school of thought, what you might call the by-election tendency, a fourth. But in these circumstances that part of the core support which didn't want to stay at home had another course of action open to it. It could vote Plaid Cymru – and it did.

In his analysis in *Wales Yearbook 2000*, the political scientist Dr. Denis Balsom shows that 38 per cent of Plaid Cymru supporters in the assembly election had voted Labour in the general election. The party got more than 28 per cent of the total vote, less than ten per cent behind Labour. In general elections in the past, despite the accumulation of four seats, they'd generally struggled at somewhere around ten per cent. This was a different kind of election and no-one can be certain of the significance of the result. It would obviously emerge in the operation of the assembly itself, but the question that still remains to be answered is whether it marked a permanent change in the nature of Welsh politics and hence in UK politics too. There's certainly no doubt that at this period Plaid Cymru took a substantial step forward in establishing itself as a significant political force in Wales. In the European Parliament elections in June 1999 the party, admittedly on a very low turnout, won two seats and was only a whisker behind Labour in its share of the overall vote. Since under 29 per cent of the population bothered to express an opinion at all, we can't be sure if the public saw this event as what you might call a proper election. Nevertheless, Plaid's progress was further underlined by the fact that, at the beginning of 2000, it could call a parliamentary by-election in Ceredigion and hold the seat with ease.

Whether this kind of advance can be sustained in Westminster elections we shall see, sooner rather than later, but if the Plaid Cymru leadership were properly brought up they'd have written a nice 'thank-you' note in recognition of the exceptional help they'd been given by Labour in the task of establishing themselves, at least for the time being, as the chief opposition party in Wales. Labour's internal troubles were a godsend in this process, but so was Labour election strategy that served mainly to give the Blaid this very status. In view of the emphasis and money Labour devotes to hiring political technocrats and their remedies, what was most striking about the party's campaign was its lack of sophistication.

It made fun of some of Plaid Cymru's sillier ambitions – a Welsh airline, a seat at the United Nations where, as Cymru, Wales would take its seat next to Cuba – but its main thrust was that here we had a separatist organisation which sought independence for Wales. This was not an unreasonable allegation, particularly as it made people like the party's president, Dafydd Wigley, very cross because he and his party also have their own private language. In it expressions like home rule, self-government, self-determination and political sovereignty do not mean what you have been brought up to think they mean.

More to the point, the voters knew perfectly well what Plaid Cymru stood for and obviously didn't care. In matters of policy and in style it was quite difficult to insert a sharpened matchstick between Plaid and Labour, each represented by respectable, middle class, social democrats almost to a man and woman (Dafydd Wigley was a Privy Councillor long before Alun Michael), and by treating them as a threat because of some far distant constitutional objective, Labour was actually endorsing the nationalists (which they also object to being called) as serious political competition.

People took the hint, even if they might not have needed one, encouraged by the fact that, if you lived in Tonypandy or Blackwood or Llanelli, there was no other political weapon available with which to give Labour a beating. It was the final element needed to create something we could now recognise as Welsh politics, as distinct from politics in Wales. It was to continue as it had begun, a compelling mixture of a little high drama and a lot of low comedy. But despite this new dimension, devolution also turned out to mean that Wales had become more rather than less significant in the scheme of British politics as a whole.

4: Alun is Returned to Sender

Labour's irrepressible enthusiasm for rigged electoral colleges underlines the fact that politicians are often slow learners. Many journalists suffer from the same deficiency and, far from excluding myself from this category, there have clearly been times when I've deserved an extended spell in the remedial class. On Sunday February 6, 2000, for example, I sat in the BBC's television studio in Crickhowell House, the headquarters of the national assembly, and said I'd be willing to bet a small amount of money on Alun Michael surviving the consequences of the vote of no confidence in him which was due to be held three days later. Not that he'd win the vote, I should say, but that losing it would not necessarily stop him going on being First Secretary.

We were hardly off the air before Lord Elis-Thomas, the assembly's Presiding Officer, offered to take the bet in the form of bottles of champagne. You'll understand from this that, although Lord Elis-Thomas is in effect the assembly's Speaker, when it comes to discretion and cautious reticence on matters of party politics, he is no Betty Boothroyd. Moments before, indeed, he'd publicly advised Alun Michael that his best course of action was to go home and pray. Anyone who knows Lord Elis-Thomas also understands that a champagne stake is very much his form of gambling.

I suppose that kind of offer from a functionary elected to maintain rigorous impartiality is one of the things they mean by the new politics. Until that moment, though, I had been convinced that the old ways of doing things would somehow prevail. In particular I believed the Labour Party would set its face against the possibility of having its choice as the leader of the assembly being picked off by a combined opposition led by Plaid Cymru. It would clearly mean a fundamental weakening in the party's authority. An alarming precedent would be set and henceforward no member of the administration would be safe in office. To insist 'Alun or no-one' would have meant an almighty constitutional crisis, but if it ended ultimately in victory for Labour, the party might have considered it to have been no bad thing. Better that than being pushed around. The principle was summed up by some of the more experienced Labour members: "We are not having the Nats telling us who our leader is going to be."

But that, as it turned out, was exactly what they were having, and ultimately they weren't nearly as unhappy at the outcome as you might have expected.

To some extent I had based my flawed analysis of events on the precedent of Christine Gwyther, the hapless Agriculture Secretary. The previous autumn the assembly had passed a motion of no confidence in her and there were no consequences of any kind. Of course the constitutional relationship between the First Secretary and the assembly was not the same, but the Gwyther experience suggested that even a minority administration might be able to face down the gesture politics of the other parties. But a rather deeper analysis of Christine's story actually reveals many of the things that were to go wrong with the Alun Michael regime and with the assembly itself.

Most people outside Pembrokeshire, where she lived and worked, and many inside the county come to that, had never heard of Christine Gwyther when she was appointed to Alun Michael's Cabinet. Still, few other members of the assembly had troubled the public imagination up to that point, and we would have to wait a while to discover exactly how interesting they were individually. But there was one exciting aspect to Christine's life and character which emerged unexpectedly after a few days: she was a vegetarian.

In any job other than that of Agriculture Secretary, this small fact would have passed without comment. Indeed, it would have been considered incorrect, even rude, to draw attention to it. But this was a time when agriculture was in turmoil, in Wales as much as anywhere else in the United Kingdom, and more than anything in the sectors which produced meat, something Christine, as a matter of principle, refused to eat. You didn't have to have a degree in marketing to recognise she was not the ideal ambassador for the lamb chop.

The idea that it might be something of an embarrassment wasn't lost on a senior Labour figure who knew Christine well. On the day of her appointment he rang the Welsh Office to tell

Alun Michael, 'in case he didn't know'. He didn't speak to Alun himself but to his private secretary, and the message was passed on. What he clearly recognised was that there was a lot of potential political damage in the appointment, whether or not Alun was already aware of Christine's views.

These days there's no particular reason why he should have known. Vegetarianism has lost most of its overtones of faddism and crankiness, the obsessive practice of people in home-made sandals to whom a lentil is kitchen heaven. In any case, many people who haven't adopted abstention as a matter of principle choose to eat meat only rarely. It's no longer a matter for explanation over the cafeteria lunch table, particularly among the health-conscious middle classes who like to think they've discovered the diet which will allow them to live for ever.

Alun says unequivocally that he did know. So instead of being accused of not doing his homework, an unlikely deficiency in any reading of his career, he can be criticised for poor political judgement. Because of the circumstances of the time Christine Gwyther was to be the most prominent single member of the Cabinet in its first months in office. She was an unimpressive performer whose public image was inevitably coloured by those private beliefs that her opponents found themselves unable to ignore. In the end Alun was more the victim than she was but, since her appointment was his responsibility, that's pretty much as it should be.

Politicians constructing administrations have always been involved in a form of balancing act (between Left and Right in the Labour Party not all that long ago, for instance). In Wales, among the plates you have to keep spinning at the end of their sticks are geography, sex and language, with ability not necessarily being a decisive factor. You've got to have representatives from all parts of Wales, you've got to have a certain number of women, there have to be some Welsh speakers. So, for example, Tom Middlehurst, from Clwyd, was put in charge of Welsh language policy even though he didn't speak Welsh. But the point here, despite the criticisms made of his appointment at the time, was that he was not opposed to the Welsh language, he did not have a principled objection, or any other objection, to its promotion. In fact some people argued that such a person might well bring more understanding and strategic ability to the question in a country where four out of five people are in exactly his position. But a *vegetarian*, in charge of *agriculture*? It wasn't funny but it was bound to become a persistent joke. You might as well put a Catholic priest on the French letter counter in Boots, they said among other things. It couldn't do anything but breed antagonism, or become the source of opposition – all the worse for being unvoiced or, even more disreputably, provide the opportunity for ceremonial and insincere disclaimers which served to draw attention to the offence they ostensibly deplored: "I'm not criticising Christine because she's a vegetarian...". It was an expression we were to hear frequently in the coming months.

As is often the way of these things, it turned out to be Christine, a woman not over-blessed with what are known as presentational skills, and already the object of unwelcome and damaging publicity, who was to be the key figure in revealing the assembly's central dilemma. Sixty men and women were being employed as full-time, professional politicians but they didn't have the faintest idea of what they might do or how they might do it.

An early idea was to end, unilaterally in Wales, the ban on the sale of beef on the bone, introduced throughout the UK as one of the measures aimed at preventing more cases of Creutzfeldt-Jacob Disease, generally described as the human variant of mad cow disease, itself officially known as BSE, otherwise bovine spongiform encephalopathy. This seemed like a particularly good idea because popular opinion said the ban was pointless and simply fuss-pot interference imposed by a nanny state against the interests of individual freedom. Trying to end the ban in Wales was a good way of sucking up to the farmers and, even better, although in itself a modest measure, it was something within the power of the assembly to decide. So, the argument went, let's decide it.

It was here that the members came up against their first, unwelcome, experience of real life. The advice from the Chief Medical Officer for Wales, Dr. Ruth Hall, was that the ban should not be lifted until further scientific evidence became available. Now it appeared that the decision was not quite as simple as various macho policy-makers, in particular the Tories, had implied. In a world of blame culture, who would be willing to ignore expert advice when one lethal incident involving a T-bone steak would be a political disaster? Not, we discovered, the members of the National Assembly for Wales.

If this decision could be seen as a responsible piece of self-restraint and common sense, it was a rare appearance for qualities which were strikingly absent when it came to matters which were more directly concerned with the condition of Welsh agriculture. There was a serious problem and the assembly could do nothing about it. Frustration turned to anger, anger to a search for victims. In order to pursue them the assembly proceeded to invent virtual politics.

Undeterred by namby-pamby questions of legality and authority, opposition parties demanded specific schemes to help livestock farmers who were, undeniably, in the unforgiving grip of an economic crisis. The Tories in particular seemed to lose touch with reality at least twice a day and apparently couldn't understand why the assembly wasn't exercising powers it didn't possess and which, as it happened, they had fought resolutely to prevent it having.

In public at least the Conservatives, most notably in the person of their leader Nick Bourne, seemed to live in a permanent state of over-excitement, a condition which led them at one stage to follow the demands of the Red Queen in *Alice's Adventures in Wonderland*: "Sentence first – verdict afterwards". This at least was the only explanation for their decision, in September 1999, to put down a motion of no confidence in Christine Gwyther before they'd actually heard what she planned to do. Their view was that she hadn't done enough for agriculture, whatever enough might have amounted to and regardless of whether or not she had the power to do it.

In keeping with the surreal nature of these events, Christine announced that she would be introducing, at a cost of £750,000, a support scheme which would, over a short period, pay £20 a head for unwanted male calves. What was more, Wales would be demonstrating its ability and will to act independently because Nick Brown, the Agriculture Minister, was refusing to bring in a similar scheme for England. Hooray, everyone said (apart from the Tories, who persisted with their motion of no confidence), action at last. That was all they knew. Less than a month later Christine was back, this time explaining that, no, actually, there wouldn't be a calf support scheme after all. Franz Fischler, the European Agriculture Commissioner, had said it was entirely against the rules of the European Union and that was the end of that. Except, as we'd come to expect, for the opposition parties who had once again been brought face to face with the impotence of the assembly. All they could do was behave like the man who kicks the cat when he's been bitten by the dog: attack Christine for the actions of Franz Fischler, a person over whom she had no control or influence. It was time for censure motion No. 2.

Dafydd Wigley opened his speech by saying it had nothing to do with the fact that Christine Gwyther was a vegetarian and/or a woman, thus guaranteeing that everyone would assume it was. Just in case you missed the point, Nick Bourne said very much the same thing. Christine herself, despite continuing her passable imitation of a blancmange, had already made it clear she had no intention of resigning, whatever the result of the vote. Alun (who was characteristically unwilling to allow his Agriculture Secretary to speak for herself) said that Christine was totally brilliant and, in particular, her performance vindicated his judgement in appointing her. No-one laughed. The motion of censure was passed and Christine didn't resign. More than that she had become, for the time being at least, unsackable. The Conservatives, clearly working off just the one brain cell, put down a motion of censure against Alun Michael. No-one supported them. Detached observers felt this was no way to run a railroad.*

*In May the following year Nick Bourne, clearly a man whose political strategy extends only to a single idea, launched yet another censure motion against the Agriculture Secretary, this time over genetically modified crops and once again her failure to do what she did not have the power to do. He did so despite it being clear that he would get no support from any other party. He must have been surprised, in the debate that followed, to have been trounced by Christine who roasted him for what she saw as his personal prejudice against her in particular and women in general. She herself lasted only until July, however, when she was abruptly sacked by Rhodri Morgan, by then First Secretary, on the eve of the Royal Welsh Show, the biggest event in the Welsh agricultural calendar.

Detached observers also felt at the time that perhaps this was a necessary testing out of rules and relationships in an organisation where, because of the arithmetic, the administration could be defeated at any time but where there was no provision for the traditional consequence of such a defeat at Westminster – a general election. However people voted in the chamber, the present assembly had somehow to continue its business until May 2003.

It was, too, the natural outcome of an uncertainty in the minds of many of the members as to what they could do to make a difference, how they could imprint their influence on life in Wales. The short answer was that they couldn't. They couldn't pass laws and they couldn't raise money, two of the prerequisites for the exercise of political power. And while they might be nominally in charge of a budget of £8 billion a year, practically all of it was spoken for one way or another for spending on essential services – health and education, for example. The grim prospect opened up of spending day after day considering the significance of, for example, the Optometrists (Variation of fees) (Wales) Order, and other pieces of what's known as secondary legislation, something that in reality required the attention of no-one much more elevated than a lone teenager armed with a rubber stamp.

So even a few months later it was possible to see how a pattern was being established, the political equivalent of lads (and some tough girls, too, believe me) on the street looking for a bit of aggro. That it had a rather more dramatic outcome than we might have expected was perhaps due as much to the complicity of the victim as to the malevolence of the people who gave him a good going-over. 'He was asking for it, wasn't he?' they might have said in one of those *East Enders* moments.

In the first place the agriculture fiasco raised any number of questions about the abilities of the administration in general and Alun Michael in particular. The Ministry of Agriculture, Fisheries and Food knew perfectly well that the calf disposal scheme being proposed for Wales was almost certain to be blocked by the European Commission. Far from making a secret of this view, the minister, Nick Brown, said as much on Radio Wales and, no doubt, elsewhere. There was absolutely no provision within the rules for such a scheme to be introduced for a part of a member country. It's inconceivable that assembly agriculture officials didn't know this too, and that they didn't pass on the advice. In these circumstances it's political suicide to say that you think you've got a good chance of getting the scheme accepted when every indication is that you won't even be asked to sit down when you arrive in Brussels.

Then again, Alun Michael is no novice (as he likes to explain regularly and at length) so why did circumstances arise in which Christine Gwyther was left twisting in the wind, humiliated by Brussels and branded as someone who promised the assembly a measure she could not deliver? Why would a politician of his maturity expose an inexperienced colleague to a serious mauling by the opposition parties? In turn that becomes an even more baffling question when you consider that Alun's persistent interference in the work of his Cabinet colleagues was greatly resented. He clearly didn't believe anything very much should happen without him being publicly at the centre of it, the man in control. During his period in office he was in many ways the Labour Party's version of a multi-purpose gadget. Nothing happened that he didn't announce it, open it, make a statement about it, answer questions about it or defend it or commend it in a speech. If he could have taken stones out of horses' hooves he would have been a boy scout knife.

In the Labour group they still talk in terms of disbelief about his obsession with detail and his insistence on making decisions himself. Cabinet colleagues would deliver public speeches from texts covered in alterations written in Alun's familiar black felt-tip pen. Assembly members who wrote to specific cabinet secretaries got their replies from Alun. When the assembly sought a new chairman for an important public body Alun sat through the interviews and later over-ruled the recommendation made by the panel concerned, a group chaired, coincidentally, by Christine Gwyther. All of which, if you didn't know politicians, might make it the more surprising that he didn't offer himself as the guilty party in the great agricultural disaster.

One of the most important aspects of this farming argument was that it set an important precedent for the opposition parties. When Christine returned empty-handed from Brussels they acted as though it simply wasn't true. They were, in the psychiatric jargon, 'in denial'. Instead of cursing the iniquities of the European Union, Plaid Cymru said the administration simply had to introduce a calf support scheme anyway, which it clearly could not do. Of course it's not that Plaid Cymru didn't understand this, but that it and the other opposition parties had stumbled on one of the devices much favoured by the Militant Tendency when it was trying to take control of the Labour Party. It's known as 'impossibilism' and it consists of instructing the party leadership (or the government or whatever) to achieve a goal which everyone is aware it cannot accomplish. When the inevitable failure is reported, the wretched functionaries concerned are denounced as traitors and lackeys and removed from office. It was a tactic which was to play an important part in the events of the following few months.

The chosen instrument was Objective One funding, the exact details of which are not required for an understanding of what happened, but which Welsh politicians treated as the European Union equivalent of the philosopher's stone. It was something that would, at the wave of a commissioner's wallet, transform the economic prospects of the great swathes of industrial and rural Wales whose deprived condition qualified them for a share of well over a billion pounds-worth of Euro-dosh. All well and good, you might think, and assembly members chattered excitedly about the new dawn that was about to break over the citizens of Merthyr Tydfil, Aberystwyth and many other places where they were having a hard time.

But there is a darkness in the Welsh psyche which also makes people deeply wary about anything that looks like good news. Gloom is our natural condition. After all, where else but Wales could you start an argument, as Dafydd Wigley did, over whether bankrupt farmers were better or worse off than redundant miners? Perhaps the Objective One money was a mistake; maybe other people were getting more than us; it wasn't enough; its value was diminishing day by day as the Euro continued its journey down the exchange rate pan. Celebration turned to anguish as old tribalisms welled up: a London government wasn't going to put itself out to make sure it actually happened. At the last minute it would surely be snatched away from under our noses.

It was this final suspicion that went to the heart of the matter, and not entirely without reason. To put it at its simplest, in order to get the EU to release the cash, it was necessary for the government to provide an equivalent amount to fund the specific projects which would be underwritten by the scheme. This general principle, which takes a number of forms in the EU, is designed to ensure that a government is not simply grabbing what it can to save its own resources. The form of words preferred by Welsh politicians was 'match funding', and it soon became a catchphrase, in the manner of old radio programmes – in this case the ironic refrain of Mona Lott in *ITMA*: "It's being so cheerful as keeps me going".

Now it's well known that the Treasury doesn't like this basic principle, holding as it does the fixed belief that all Euromoney is really British and the various Euro grant schemes are simply methods of restoring it to its rightful owners. It would almost certainly have been looking deeply into various ways of getting its hands on the Objective One cash without adding a penny piece of its own to the total. From this point, if you are a Welsh opposition politician, it's not even a short bus ride to the unshakeable belief that the government is working out how to deprive you of the prize on which you have set your heart. As the man said in *M*A*S*H*: "I'm only paranoid because everyone's against me".

More significantly, it was an early manifestation of an argument which was always widely forecast to be an inevitable consequence of the devolution arrangement. Anything that went wrong, or appeared to go wrong, was, by definition, the fault of the government at Westminster. In the most important matters the assembly was simply a client of that government. So the question became whether the assembly could find a method of compelling the Blair regime to do what it would not otherwise do. It was at the centre of the new relationship between Cardiff and London.

It was at this point that the shoehorning of Alun Michael into the job of First Secretary took on a new and even greater significance. In the first place its negative influence on the assembly election result meant Labour was in a minority and so could not lurk behind a numerical barrier as the whooping hordes of Plaid

Cymru and other opposition parties fired arrows at the Labour stockade. But Alun was also the man Tony Blair had urged on the Welsh public as "a great guy", which is Downing Street shorthand for semi-divine. In that case, opposition politicians argued mischievously, it would be a simple matter for Alun to use his much-vaunted influence in London to persuade the Chancellor, Gordon Brown, to give an unbreakable promise that the necessary support was on its way. After all, ministers, including Blair, went round saying they "wouldn't let Wales down". In that case it was surely only a modest concession, if a concession at all, to demonstrate that commitment in the form of hard cash.

But to make this strategy effective, it had to be taken a stage further. The opposition parties needed to name a specific sum of money that had to be handed over, and a specific day on which the Securicor lorry, with its cargo of used ten pound notes, had to arrive from Whitehall. Choosing a deadline was simple enough. The assembly had to give final approval to its budget on Tuesday, February 8. If the necessary money were not included in that budget then the opposition would launch a motion of no confidence in the First Secretary. Shrewdly, they played it long, announcing this intention before Christmas, allowing the screw to turn and public expectation to grow. Plaid Cymru members took the leading role and put themselves in a position where they could not lose. If the money turned up it would demonstrate the influence they could bring to bear as they battled for a fair deal for Wales against a grudging administration passing on second-hand policies made in London. If there was no money then they'd get Alun and, through him, the Labour Party and the Government.

As for the actual amount of money considered necessary, anyone's guess was as good as anyone else's. The argument put forward was that significant resources were needed immediately to begin the Objective One process. Labour said that would be around £25 million and they had that available. There was no need to trouble the Treasury. Plaid Cymru said it was £85 million, a figure the party insisted it hadn't drawn out of thin air, although it might just as well have. The other parties agreed since they had no better means of calculation than Plaid Cymru. The truth was that we were now watching one of those ransom movies: 'Give us the money or the boy dies'.

This doesn't seem to have been a strategy which was carefully thought out by the main actors, but rather one the Plaid Cymru leadership in particular made up as it went along. The party was certainly very nervous about the course that was being taken, especially because it could well undermine even the modest reputation then enjoyed by the assembly in the eyes of the Welsh public. Nevertheless it turned out to be cleverly done and it was something from which everyone could eventually learn: how to use the limited authority of the assembly to achieve a political objective which might teach Labour a lesson. Of the four chief temptations in political life – greed, sex, alcohol and pomposity – it's perhaps the last which is the most dangerous. People who, when grudgingly given a few votes, announce to the world that they have been granted a unique insight into the most heartfelt desires of 'the people of Wales', are often unable to grasp the extent of their own self-delusion. They pose as men and women of intellectual and moral substance dealing judiciously with great affairs of state when in reality they're throwing their toys out of the pram in a bad-tempered effort to persuade someone to give them a chocolate biscuit. Hardly anyone would say that Alun Michael didn't have it coming, but no-one could argue either that the process of getting rid of him advanced the cause of Welsh politics or provided even ten pence-worth of help to the deprived areas over which they wailed so noisily.

Of course they all knew that. They didn't really think the Chancellor would suddenly adopt the economic policy of the rich uncle, handing over £85 million to young Alun so that he could buy a slap-up meal for those rough boys who were threatening to push him out of the playground. That's not how it works and they knew that wasn't how it worked. For example, what would they say on Merseyside where they were also waiting for match funding for their Objective One projects? How long would it be before another crisis blew up in Wales which Dafydd Wigley and Nick Bourne and Mike German, the Liberal Democrat leader, certified needed money now? At the same time, it has to be said, there is often a touching innocence about the average assembly member's grasp of fiscal strategy.

For example, in May 2000 Plaid Cymru became probably the only party in the entire world to call for higher levels of inflation – an idea dreamt up by Professor Phil Williams, the space scientist who doubles as the party's economic brainbox.

As far as Objective One was concerned though, the opposition had adopted the old rugby slogan: 'Never mind the ball, get on with the game', the game being getting rid of Alun Michael. After that took place, it's particularly significant to note, we didn't hear another word about the £85 million or any other specific sum of money. It was what Alfred Hitchcock called the 'MacGuffin', the otherwise trivial element in a drama which serves to set the whole plot in motion. Thus the members of the opposition parties could present themselves as men and women of zeal and principle confronting the malevolent forces of Westminster which were indifferent to the future of the people of Wales. In reality, as we know, they were a lynch mob.

They were lucky in their choice of victim since he practically went out and bought the rope for them. Not all Alun Michael's difficulties were of his own making but there he was, portrayed as a Downing Street poodle, but one whose tail-wagging had no apparent influence on his master. He had been levered into the leadership of the assembly through a disreputable device, the story went, thus cheating Rhodri Morgan, a popular figure, of what was seen as his rightful position. His predecessor as Secretary of State, Ron Davies, was going round saying how useless Alun was (especially compared to Ron, you'll understand). He was unpopular in his own group because of his insistence on doing practically everything himself; by the time of the vote of no confidence some calculations suggested that he had the support of only five of his assembly colleagues. Even worse than all those things, the political arithmetic was implacably against him: 32 opposition votes against 28 Labour. Oh, and on the Thursday before the no confidence vote, the Labour Party had come fourth in the parliamentary by-election in Ceredigion in which Plaid Cymru had had an easy victory.

When you look at these circumstances you wonder, at this distance, why he didn't save everyone a lot of trouble and chuck himself off Penarth Head. At the same time, though, there was a feeling, certainly one I shared, that something would happen to reassert the traditional system by which a governing party, even one in a minority, would not have its leader picked for it by someone else. At the national assembly, though, traditional political systems had been crucially altered. The post of First Secretary was in the gift of the assembly itself, and not in the hands of the party. If the assembly withheld its endorsement he could not serve. At the same time, as I've already mentioned, an election could not be called to resolve the impasse, as it would have been at Westminster.

There were reports that Alun himself was spending considerably more time than hitherto talking warmly to members of his own party in an effort to stiffen their resolve. And, in an even more desperate throw, he looked beyond the grave to explain that Owain Glyndwr, the fifteenth century Welsh rebel prince, would have behaved very much as he was doing. In a speech at Machynlleth at the end of January Alun said: "I like to think that Owain Glyndwr might look at the situation today and offer advice. He might say: 'I was a hero for my time: I did it my way. For your time, do it your way'."

I suspect, however, that even if Owain Glyndwr – whose death, after all, has never been confirmed despite almost six hundred years elapsing since he was last seen – had turned up at the assembly to urge everyone to back the First Secretary it would still have done no good.

Gordon Brown did his bit, such as it was. He called Welsh journalists in to No. 11 and sang the old song about not letting Wales down. It wasn't enough. I was reminded of the days when trade unionists marched through the streets chanting their wage claims. "What do we want?" "Eighty-five million pounds!" "When do we want it?" "Now!"

A Welsh Labour MP, Jon Owen Jones, explained helpfully that Alun's leadership was unpopular and that the Prime Minister was badly advised (Prime Ministers never make their own mistakes in the eyes of those who seek their patronage) to push him into the job. He, Alun, should resign. Alun had sacked Jones from his Welsh Office ministerial job the previous summer. The *Western Mail* reported: "[Mr. Jones]...said his call was not based on any personal animosity."

Tony Blair rang Charles Kennedy, the Leader of the Liberal

Democrats, and asked if his assembly members could do something to help Alun out. If it was a surprising question from a man devoted to the political machine, it got the expected answer. It was up to the Liberal Democrats in Wales to make their own decisions. Something called devolution, see. In any case, Kennedy would have got a very short answer from Cardiff. Even so, until virtually the last minute Alun and his advisers thought they might still be persuaded to do something. The night before the censure motion was to be staged he, Rhodri Morgan and Paul Murphy, the Welsh Secretary, sat in the Cabinet offices on the fifth floor of Crickhowell House, waiting for the Liberal Democrat members to make their way upstairs for a cosy chat about some kind of deal. The Lib Dems chose instead to go to a curry house in the Canton district of Cardiff, somewhere they could no doubt watch each other in case a faint whiff of office caused their less resolute AMs to crack at the last moment.

There was, though, one drama left. Not that the assembly itself had any sense of theatre, even on that day. Although it was about to take probably the most significant decision available to it, passing a vote of no confidence in the man it had elected its leader fewer than nine months earlier, it might as well have been a meeting of the footpaths committee of Trumpton Parish Council. The three opposition party leaders were allocated ten minutes each to speak on the motion, Alun twenty-five minutes to reply. There were to be no other speeches, for or against, none of the shades of argument which are usually the essence of politics. No doubt the perfunctory nature of the proceedings would allow assembly members with small children to get home in time for tea, something a number of them consider to be at the very core of the democratic process.

Well, why bother talking about it when the noose was already tied and the verdict a certainty? Alun was going to lose. The important question was what would happen after that.

In the previous weeks there had been continuing speculation that, when Alun was defeated, as he was apparently certain to be, he would simply be put up again by the Labour group. He would be voted out again and renominated, a procedure that would have brought the assembly into even greater disrepute than it was already. But since none of the other parties was prepared to put forward an alternative candidate they'd just have to go on playing ping-pong.

This was not, however, the view of the Presiding Officer, Lord Elis-Thomas, who had taken legal advice independent of that being put forward by the assembly's counsel-general, Winston Roddick QC. Dafydd El (as he is always known) was particularly concerned about the duality of the role of counsel-general since he advised both the administration and the assembly.

The Presiding Officer embarked on an arduous tour of television and radio studios, a selfless act carried out, he said, to make sure the public, the poor old voters, understood what was going on in what was, after all, an institution so new they hadn't finished taking the wrapping paper off. Only cruel observers suggested that vanity and Dafydd El's love of demonstrating his own urbane talents played any significant part in this exercise.

His message was clear enough. He would not allow repeated nominations of the same candidate. Once perhaps, maybe twice, but not to the point where the assembly imploded. His other vital decision was that there wouldn't be a long interval between elections. There would be an adjournment of an hour during which time the Labour group would have to come forward with the name of an acting First Secretary. If a further vote of no confidence emerged it would be heard the next day, rather than during the following week.

Alun Michael was furious but hemmed in. By now the Labour group was willing to demonstrate solidarity by supporting him in the first vote, but many of them would not do so after that. Because of that the only move left to him, one that he decided in private, was to try and see to it that the vote never took place at all. For the first, and probably the last, time in his political life he sprang a surprise on supporters and opponents.

It certainly appeared to take even Tony Blair unawares. At the very moment the Prime Minister was telling the House of Commons, "I believe the Welsh First Secretary is doing an excellent job," Alun was handing in his resignation. If Blair knew of his plan, which Downing Street later said was the case, it was a curious form of words to choose, not to mention an embarrassing one as Tory MPs, alerted by their pagers, gleefully shouted the news across the chamber. Then again, if he did know, perhaps it reinforces the general belief that it wasn't a real resignation at all, just Alun's last effort to save his skin. The difficulty of deciding which politician or politician's spokesman to believe at any given time was further underlined a few months later when, on Radio 4, Alun told John Humphrys that he hadn't informed Blair about his intentions. There hadn't been enough time, he said. Someone here is having difficulties with the truth and it sounds like Downing Street to me.

At this point it's necessary to choose between two distinct interpretations of that afternoon's events. The first is that Alun, man of principle, was sacrificing himself for the good of the assembly and that of the Labour Party. The other is that he had made a legalistic calculation that, if he resigned before a vote was taken, then he would not have been removed from office by a vote of no confidence and so would be free to seek re-election. I subscribe to the second version, not least because his method of resigning seemed calculated to meet a particular strategy rather than forming a dramatic gesture of farewell.

The crucial words in what was essentially a lacklustre, rather brief and subdued speech of self-defence seem to bear that out. "It cannot be right," he said, "for Plaid Cymru to choose who leads Labour. Nor is it right for the Conservatives and the Liberal Democrats to connive with that purpose. That is why I have decided to put the choice back clearly with the Labour Party by resigning as First Secretary with immediate effect."

Still speaking, and quoting the rituals of standing orders, he crossed a few feet from his rostrum to hand a letter to the Presiding Officer. In theory, it appeared, he was now no longer First Secretary and so could not be sacked from a job he didn't hold. In theory it was open to his party to re-nominate him.

A little later, journalists and politicians picked over the theology of all this. If he wasn't First Secretary, people asked, how come he was still speaking? In any case, when was the precise moment of transformation from assembly leader to humble backbencher? Was it when he handed the letter over? Was it when Lord Elis-Thomas opened it? – which he did not do immediately. Was it when Dafydd El had read it through from beginning to end? – something he resisted doing while actually presiding that day. Briefly fascinating though those questions were, they had no effect on the outcome. The Presiding Officer called the vote. There were Labour protests. The Presiding Officer looked up at the Plaid Cymru members, who sat on their hands. The motion had not been withdrawn, therefore the voting procedure must continue. Alun was out.

In fact, although it's entirely academic to say so, his manoeuvre had only transformed his position from hopeless to entirely impossible. Labour members who a few minutes before had loyally applauded him at the end of his speech were appalled that they had been given no inkling of what he planned. Even his most devoted supporters recognised that this was the end. Within the hour Rhodri Morgan had been chosen by the Labour group as acting First Secretary. The following week he was confirmed in the job.

At this stage it was possible to detect, above all, a great sense of relief. The assembly, bursting with frustration at all the things it couldn't do, had finally lashed out at its own impotence. The most significant move open to it was getting rid of Alun Michael. It had done so, and clearly felt the better for it. It was a first symbolic assertion, a message to Westminster, of the consequences of devolution. At the same time many of the tensions between opposition and administration within the assembly had been resolved for the time being, although in no sense cured. The Labour group had been handed a way out of the problem of an increasing lack of sympathy and respect between its members and its leader. Alun Michael, a capable and hard-working politician, had been the wrong man for the job.

He still thought he had somehow been the victim of dirty tricks and he grumbled in particular about the role in his downfall of Dafydd Elis-Thomas as presiding officer. Relations between the two men were chilly*, and a lot of people shared his doubts, which were later raised by the Liberal Democrats in the House of Lords. But Dafydd El, sometimes absurd (a man who, publicly accused of spending too much money on designer

---

*Just how chilly could be seen from the Presiding Officer's letter (or, more accurately, Welsh language e-mail) of farewell to the ex-First Secretary. "Dear Alun," it read, "Events did not permit me to reply properly to your letter of resignation. I would like to acknowledge your contribution to Welsh politics."

clothes, answered his critics by saying he always waited for the sales before buying them), but a man deeply skilled in the arts of political survival, seemed unperturbed as he sipped his champagne.

In any case, there was a mood to get on. As it happened, Alun's constituency of Cardiff South and Penarth had kept the seat warm, perhaps as a result of a premonition that things would go wrong. He left the assembly and returned to Westminster where, it was clear, he more properly belonged. After a few months he was restored to an inner circle of people advising Tony Blair on strategy for the next election. We were faced with one of those things so rare in real life: a series of tidy and more or less happy endings.

For no-one more so than Rhodri Morgan, whose ultimate victory was the most extraordinary outcome of a series of events which had taken on an almost fictional quality. In the public mind he had become the central figure in some kind of nineteenth-century Ruritanian romance. I kept thinking of *The Prisoner of Zenda*. Rhodri was the heir who had been unjustly kept from the throne by the sinister activities of conspirators within the palace. Now at last he had been anointed and he could take his rightful place as the leader of a grateful people.

Even Tony Blair, the arch foe who, from the safety of his Westminster fortress, had fomented opposition to Rhodri, eventually came to bend the knee in a kind of homage. "I got that judgement wrong," Blair said in a rare moment of self-doubt. "You've got to exercise discretion. You've got to know the battles to fight and the battles not to fight."

As they closed the book there were perhaps a few who wiped away a furtive, sentimental tear.

5: Rod Meets a Girl in a Pub

One of the more extraordinary aspects of Welsh politics is the way in which some of its leading figures have become victims of offences they haven't committed. Ron Davies is the outstanding example, of course, but the former leader of the Welsh Conservatives, Rod Richards, is in very much the same category. What Rod *didn't* do was assault a young woman, but his innocence, endorsed by a British jury, seemed unlikely to be enough to save him from the political oblivion with which he had flirted for so long. It was perhaps revealing that, unusually in these sort of circumstances, no friends and supporters were seen rallying round to pronounce it 'a personal tragedy'. But then, popularity with his colleagues was never one of Rod's more pressing problems.

In the rather flat landscape presented by Welsh politicians in general, Rod is an unexpected figure. He served in the Royal Marines on a short service commission, and at various times was an economist, television researcher, newsreader, publican, ministerial adviser, Member of Parliament and Welsh Office minister, as well as having in the background some necessarily shadowy connections with the world of intelligence and security. Over the years that pluralistic background was reflected, sometimes dramatically, in the erratic course of his journey through public life, although he could hardly be picked out from the crowd by the fact that some of his more spectacular troubles arose from difficulties with girls.

In the summer of 1996, for example, everything was going smoothly enough. He'd been a junior minister at the Welsh Office since 1994 and, as MP for Clwyd West, he held the safest Tory seat in Wales. While no-one was predicting a notably glittering future for him, there seemed to be no particular reason why he shouldn't enjoy a long and comfortable career in the relatively undemanding world of Welsh politics.

If there was a problem which caused some public comment it arose from his peculiarly combative nature: unlike many of his colleagues, when he was rude he sounded as though he meant it. He gave the clear impression that he had a deep personal grudge against the objects of his scorn, people who were later to include many ostensibly on his own side. He had, it must be said, an unconcealed appreciation of his own talents and an unswerving taste for directing loud sarcasm at anyone who disagreed with him. On one occasion, for example, he described Welsh Labour councillors as "short, fat, slimy and fundamentally corrupt" ("Hey, less of the short," one councillor complained) – a remark so lacking in any redeeming sense of irony or lightness of tone that even John Redwood, then the Welsh Secretary, felt obliged to reprimand him for it.

'Robust' is the politest word used for the kind of confrontation in which Rod specialised, although some people preferred to describe him as grotesquely offensive. Whatever the adjective, his abrasive manner accounted for the distinct lack of sympathy that greeted his abrupt departure from office in the summer of 1996, one of a series of Conservative MPs discovered in sexual misconduct of one kind or another. By the standards established before and afterwards by some of his colleagues (pregnant mistresses, affairs with teenagers, lovemaking while wearing football kit, three-in-a-bed 'romps' and the rest of it, real and rumoured) the behaviour attributed to Rod seemed straightforward enough. But the mood of the times meant that within hours of a Sunday paper carrying stories about him, the bed, the silk scarves and 'PR girl' Julia Felthouse, he was clearing his desk at the Welsh Office.

So far, so average Tory MP, you might have thought, and while Rod, like Ron Davies, is not the kind of person to linger too long over acts of contrition, it turned out that the Felthouse affair, on which he never commented publicly, was to be simply the first of a series of events through which he conducted a lengthy tutorial on how not to maintain a career in modern politics.

In May the following year he lost his Westminster seat. He failed to win it back in another form at the assembly elections two years later, but nevertheless got into the assembly through the additional member system. Later, the Conservatives of Clwyd West chose someone else as their parliamentary candidate. In August 1999, having been charged with causing grievous bodily harm to a girl he'd met in a pub, he had to resign as leader of the Welsh Conservatives. He had intended that to be a temporary standing aside, but his assembly colleagues, with a single exception, could hardly believe their luck and, seizing their chance, rushed to make the resignation permanent.

The following February, on the day Alun Michael was forced out of office, the Conservatives in the assembly staged a curtain-raiser by chucking Rod out of their group because, they said, he'd disobeyed the party whip by abstaining rather than voting against the assembly budget. Generalised discontent with his behaviour and his manner was perhaps an even more important motive in their decision. Rod underlined why that might have been so when, at an informal press conference moments later, he announced that he was "the real Welsh Conservative Party", and described Nick Bourne, his successor as leader, as "a complete prat".

On the face of it, things took a turn for the better when he was acquitted of causing grievous bodily harm to 23-year-old Cassandra Melvin (she said he'd broken her arm, he said she'd attacked him) whom he'd met with her sister at a pub in Richmond. But even innocence had its price. Asked in court if he'd had thoughts of a sexual encounter with the women (with whom he had earlier dined on pizzas) Rod, who was thirty years older than Ms. Melvin, replied: "Yes perhaps that was a possibility I still haven't ruled out and there was no reason in my domestic arrangements why I should not pursue that."

It was an answer that proved rather too much for Liz, otherwise Mrs. Rod Richards, who did not like the implication that she was perfectly happy to allow her husband to behave pretty much as he pleased in this regard. A couple of weeks later she featured in a two-page interview in the *Daily Mail* saying that not only did she no longer live with Rod, of whom she painted an unflattering portrait, but that she intended to divorce him.

And there was one other bit of bad news for the wayward Tory. Shortly after his acquittal on the GBH charge, the brewers Whitbread began bankruptcy proceedings against him over debts of £200,000 connected with his days as a publican. The bankruptcy petition was later to be dismissed by the High Court, but in the circumstances the publicity was hardly helpful.

Well, as the lawyers say, hard cases make bad law. While none of these incidents and events was particularly edifying, it makes you wonder how much such things really matter. We live in a world where the new puritanism, inflamed by over-excited journalism, has demanded ever more unrealistic standards of behaviour from politicians whose otherwise pedestrian character is often demonstrated by the low-grade nature of their sins. Rod Richards can hardly be described as leading a blameless life, but in this he's no different from large numbers of his Welsh political contemporaries and predecessors.

It's also a world in which it's virtually impossible to decide which virtues and which flaws are significant and which are simply the frailties visited upon all of us in one form or another as symptoms of our humanity. On the one hand, promiscuity, drug-taking, drunkenness, infidelity and greed are advertised as the indispensable, and somehow admirable, preoccupations of rock musicians or film actors. On the other, newspapers shriek that a Member of Parliament who commits adultery should be shunned by all right-thinking people.

A man who would lie to his wife, columnists say, is perfectly capable of lying to the country. They prefer to ignore the fact that many politicians who lie to the country may well tell the truth to their wives. It seems to me that a much more interesting aspect of this debate is whether it is something in the nature of politics which provokes a certain amount of instability in this and other areas; whether a political career is particularly attractive to people with flexible moral standards and powerful physical needs.

I have certainly known many MPs whose sexual energy was apparently prodigious. Other men usually have to rely on circumstantial or second-hand evidence to make such judgements, of course, but conversations with women colleagues often have a convincingly repetitive ring to them. A typical exchange might go like this:

> Man journalist: "What about... (name of Welsh MP)?"
> Woman journalist 1: "I've had a lot of trouble with him."
> Woman journalist 2: "Hasn't everybody?"
> Woman journalist 1: "He's desperate."

Some have reputations as being difficult to get rid of. Others proposition women routinely, apparently trying their luck. Even the most outwardly respectable and mature of them, deacon-faced, indulge from time to time in those sly, Nonconformist gropes they hope are ambiguous enough to pass unchallenged by the victim. Many are apparently convinced that a lustre of power shimmers from the surface of even the most unappetising backbench MP that makes him irresistible to girls.

Quite frequently this kind of activity is the consequence of a second failing to which politicians (yes, I know, and journalists) are particularly prone: drink. I'm under the impression that this particular vice is much less popular than it was a generation ago. Heavy drinking, once part of the macho occupational culture of both politics and journalism, is no longer looked upon with tolerant benevolence by the relevant authorities.

It's happened throughout the working world. The cocktail cabinets in the corners of executive offices remain locked. The fridges contain only mineral water in fancy bottles. In the corporate world a second tomato juice taken at a meal is seen as the sign of an addictive personality. The long lunch has been abandoned in favour of the working breakfast. The chief executive chews on a banana rather than a big cigar.

The two trades of politics and journalism were once particularly susceptible to the temptations of booze because, among other things, they both involved hanging around late in the day with nothing very much to do. A quarter of a century ago there were plenty of MPs who were incoherent by half past two in the afternoon and blotto by nightfall. For some people politics was as much a kind of hobby as it was a job. They could get as ratted as they liked as long as they were capable of stumbling through the voting lobbies at the appropriate time.

Years ago, a friend of mine, a successful politician, was deeply offended when his capacity for drink was brought into question. Filling in an application for life insurance his doctor got to the question about alcohol consumption.

"What shall we put you down for? Three pints a day?"

The MP was outraged. "Don't be daft. More like twelve."

But there we are, doctors seem to drink a lot less these days, too.

Nowadays perhaps politics is an occupation that more closely mirrors the preoccupations of the outside world, and the kind of corporate philosophy which characterises business has substantially influenced the behaviour of MPs. They now see themselves as middle managers, perhaps in the public relations department, in that great enterprise which runs the United Kingdom. If they keep their noses clean they might aspire to promotion, even to the board of the company itself. In the light of this professionalising of the trade it pays to be industrious, dull and safe, to draw attention to yourself only by your eagerness to please.

No-one is suggesting that MPs should attempt to restore the old standards of boozing as a demonstration of their independence of spirit, but the caution which informs much of their conduct is also encouraged by their awareness that any form of misbehaviour will not simply be something known only to other members of the political club. It will also be passed on to the voters by the newspapers.

We know now, for instance, that Churchill drank like a fish, sipping away all day. Another Prime Minister, H.H. Asquith, who wrote letters to his girlfriend during Cabinet meetings, was known as Squiffy, partly as a version of his name, but also as a reference to his heavy drinking. Harold Wilson increasingly took to fortifying himself with brandy before facing Prime Minister's questions on Tuesday and Thursday afternoons. In the hands of today's journalists these men would at the very least have faced difficult questions about their fitness for office. But even as late as the sixties George Brown's persistent and public drunkenness (he seemed to be able to get drunk and become sober several times on the same day) led to no particular clamour for him to be sacked as Foreign Secretary. On one occasion, indeed, the *Times* carried a leader that declared: "Better George Brown drunk than Harold Wilson sober."

In general, though, there was until comparatively recently a reticence about the private behaviour of politicians which, on an occasion on which it was threatened, led three leading Labour politicians to take extraordinary steps to maintain it.

One of them was Aneurin Bevan, a man whose name still inspires so much awe in Wales that, forty years after his death, a highly successful rock group, the Manic Street Preachers, still took inspiration from him. Bevan's private life was always the object of sensational and detailed speculation. It arose chiefly from a burning desire to catch a leading politician indulging in the deadliest of sins: hypocrisy. When he came to visit his constituency of Ebbw Vale, people said, he would get out of a massive limousine at Newport and travel the rest of the way in some small and elderly saloon. Or, in another version, he would go into the lavatory on the train to change from his smart London suit into something shabbier and hence more suitable for the Monmouthshire valleys.

All this was nonsense, of course, and in any case there was no particular secret about the fact that Bevan enjoyed good living. It was why the Tory minister, Brendan Bracken, called him a Bollinger Bolshevik. Bevan just laughed and saw no reason why a socialist should wear a hair shirt.

In 1957, though, it appeared that there was a limit to how much gossip and innuendo he was prepared simply to shrug off. The occasion was the conference of the Italian Socialist Party held in Venice in February of that year. Bevan went with Morgan Phillips, the Welshman who was then general secretary of the Labour Party, and Richard Crossman, later to be a cabinet minister under Harold Wilson. At that time Crossman was a journalist as well as an MP.

The behaviour of the three men was later described in an article in the *Spectator* by the journalist Jenny Nicholson. "And then there was the occasional appearance of Messrs Bevan, Morgan Phillips and Richard Crossman... [They] puzzled the Italians by their capacity to fill themselves like tanks with whisky and coffee while they (because of their livers and also because they are abstemious by nature) were keeping going on mineral water and an occasional coffee. Although the Italians were never sure if the British delegation was sober, they always attributed to them an immense political acumen."

Although the article doesn't specifically say the men were drunk, it's difficult to come up with any other convincing explanation for this description, however cautiously phrased it was. The three politicians got their lawyers to write to *The Spectator* saying they had been the subjects of a serious libel. While that might have been at least partly true, it did not apply to Morgan Phillips. Crossman wrote in his diary, published posthumously fourteen years later, that Phillips was "tiddly by mid-day and soaked by dinner-time." He also said that Phillips had been "dead drunk for most of the conference". Long after the event, the journalist Auberon Waugh reported that Crossman had told him that he and Bevan had been "pissed as newts".

Whatever the exact state of each individual participant, it was clearly a huge risk to go to court over the matter. Nevertheless they sued, and were each awarded £2,500 (enough to buy a decent house in 1957). Defenders of Bevan and Crossman have found it necessary to go rather deeply into the detail of the affair to excuse their conduct. Michael Foot has argued that Bevan was much more likely to have drunk wine rather than the whisky described in the article. The same point is made about Crossman by his biographer, Anthony Howard, who also says that the expression "pissed as newts" was highly uncharacteristic. Auberon Waugh now says that he might well have put those exact words into Crossman's mouth, but that the politician's message was unambiguous. In any case, these are not things that deal with the real burden of the story: whether they lied and made a profit by doing so.

In strict legal terms the three men may not have committed perjury but it's difficult to avoid the impression that they were guilty of its moral equivalent. The action implied that they were all – Morgan Phillips included – sober throughout. That was clearly not so and for that reason the incident, which became known in the Labour Party as the Venetian blind, is a useful reminder of the moments of weakness that can sweep over even the most distinguished and ostensibly clear-sighted politicians.

Sometimes this kind of moral blindness seems to seize an entire generation so that its members come to believe that a particular course of conduct, although officially outside the rules, is sanctioned by a general acceptance of it: like driving at more than seventy miles an hour on a motorway. Yes, it's illegal, the argument goes, but no-one really cares and if they prosecuted everyone doing more than seventy the police wouldn't have time to carry out any other duties.

It seems to me that that's the message in the story of Keith

Best, the Conservative who unexpectedly became MP for Anglesey in 1979 and, just as unexpectedly, was sent to gaol in 1987. It was a career in which he was both a beneficiary and a victim of Thatcherism.

Best was a bouncy young man of not quite thirty when he won Anglesey. The constituency had been either Liberal or Labour throughout the century and neither he nor his party seemed likely to disturb that tradition. It was true that there were political changes taking place in Welsh-speaking rural Wales, but the benefit had gone to Plaid Cymru which by this time held three seats. The circumstances of the election were certainly against Labour. It had been called by an exhausted government, discredited in particular by the Winter of Discontent, and which had also just undergone a four-to-one hammering in the referendum which decided whether or not there should be an elected Welsh assembly. Emphatically not.

It's true, too, that Anglesey was particularly vulnerable at this time. Cledwyn Hughes (now Lord Cledwyn of Penrhos) had been the MP since 1951, one of the group of Welsh Labour politicians who had been so influential in the Labour Party during the sixties and seventies. He had been Welsh Secretary and Agriculture Secretary and later a long-serving chairman of the Parliamentary Labour Party. Perhaps his record and his distinction disguised the way in which the constituency was changing. For example, substantial numbers of English people had chosen to retire to the island. Even so, while in general many people in rural Wales are very conservative in their attitudes, there was no sign at that time they were inclined to *vote* Conservative.

In these circumstances it seemed unlikely that a young (and looking younger), non-Welsh-speaking, unmarried, English barrister was going to overturn Anglesey's traditions. What seems to have happened was that he slipped through a window of time at which Labour was in decline in the constituency but Plaid Cymru had not yet made a substantial impact as it was to do later, thanks in part at least to Keith Best's misfortunes.

In 1979 you might have though Best was a bit too cherubic, a bit too breezy perhaps, to be treated seriously as a politician. But he was also energetic and conscientious and an indefatigable advocate for the island, never too busy to give a speech, or pronounce on this and that through the Welsh media. These are all essential qualities in insecure constituencies and they quickly made Best a fixture on the Welsh political landscape.

All that boyish bustle and chubby, curly-haired charm gave him an air of innocence that some people suggested, as people do in the world of politics, was too good to be true. And that was to be the central question asked over his spectacular downfall: was he a helpless victim of his own naïveté or a pioneer of sleaze, the first in a long line of Tories who thought the rules didn't apply to them?

Best had already won a second election by the time those aspects of economic policy most closely identified with Thatcherism had begun to move smoothly from philosophy into practice. One of the most important ideas was to put the government at a greater distance from industry, commerce and employment. There were two related methods used to achieve this objective. One was reform of the legislation that applied to trades unions; the other was a reduction of the public sector, in particular through a process of privatisation. In its most seductive form that created the feeling that somehow the government had invented an infallible method by which people could get rich, or at least enjoy a modest windfall.

Nowhere was that more attractive an idea than in the sell-off in 1984 of British Telecom for £4 billion. Everyone knew that here was a no-risk purchase since the government had to market the shares at an attractive (i.e. below real value) price to make sure they were bought. It wasn't a question of people being given an opportunity to make money, they *had* to make money if the principle were to be advertised as yet another brilliant wheeze by Mrs. Thatcher and the geniuses who surrounded her.

Under these circumstances anyone who knew the first thing about the stock market (in the main people who were already involved in buying and selling equities) would have been a mug if he'd failed to get his hands on as many shares as possible. The frustrating thing was that the government, in an effort to see that share ownership and the benefits of privatisation were spread as widely as possible, imposed a strict limit on the number of shares any individual could be allocated: in the case of British Telecom it was eight hundred.

The whole privatisation process was so huge that it's obvious many people thought that this regulation was simply a minor obstacle and, more than anything, a test of their ingenuity. The share register ran to fifty thousand pages containing two million names. The chances of multiple applications being detected were obviously slim. But that was to ignore the fact that there is always someone out there in an anorak who will dedicate himself to proving that establishment figures, particularly Conservative MPs, are greedier than they are cautious.

Neil Moister, of *Labour Research* magazine, decided to comb through the microfiche of the names of people who had bought shares to see who was up to what. It was something that demanded dogged determination as line after line of the millions of names scrolled up the small screen in front of him. With today's information technology he could probably have found what he was looking for within minutes. But he had a bit of luck, thanks to the alphabet.

Best's name, for obvious reasons, was high up the list. So were the variations of it (his full name is Keith Lander Best). It emerged soon enough that, using various addresses and bank accounts, he'd got six times more shares than he was legally entitled to. If he'd been called Keith Williams perhaps the indefatigable Moister wouldn't have reached him before his eyesight gave out.

Although the privatisation of British Telecom took place in 1984, it wasn't until three years later that Best's transgression was made public. The Labour Party naturally made a tremendous fuss and demanded that he should resign. At the same time the Conservative Party adopted the high moral tone we were to get used to when it came to errant Members of Parliament. Best himself recalled later that the whips advised him "...to keep a low profile, stay out of the chamber of the House of Commons and it would all blow over".

It didn't blow over, though, not least because there was a general election around the corner and Labour had good reasons for not losing interest. In the end, on the specific instructions of the then party chairman, Norman Tebbitt, Best had to stand down from Anglesey. At the May election the seat was won for Plaid Cymru by Ieuan Wyn Jones, although the figures suggest that he might have been successful in any case, scandal or no scandal.

Even then that wasn't the end of it for Best. For reasons that are unclear, he was prosecuted (although another Conservative MP who had done much the same thing was not) and at Southwark Crown Court, where he wept in the witness box, he was sentenced to four months in gaol.

In the event, he spent only a few days in Brixton Prison before being released when an appeal hearing substituted a larger fine. That was about the only favour anyone did him. His career was wrecked. He could no longer earn a living as a barrister, he was forced to resign his commission in the Territorial Army, he was unemployable.

There are, though, a number of morals in this story, apart from the obvious one, and, for once, an upbeat ending. Unable to get any work, Best helped out voluntarily for a charity. That led to a paid job working for British people held in prisons abroad. From there he became chief executive of another charity, the Immigration Advisory Service, guiding clients through the fog of regulation that often overwhelms those seeking to settle in the United Kingdom. He became as cheerful and energetic in this work as he ever was as an MP. He might well have felt, too, that by chance he had discovered a more useful role in life. Released from the treadmill of politics, he found time to marry and have two daughters, to whom he is devoted.

When asked, he is rueful about the foolishness that led to his downfall, but it is a rare thing outside old-fashioned fiction to discover someone who has found redemption through good works. The only people who seem to manage to find this anything other than admirable are those who run the Conservative Party. In the summer of 2000, long after these events, they made it clear Best wouldn't be welcome as a possible candidate in Anglesey, where he retained a house, spent many holidays and practised his Welsh. That was despite the enthusiasm of some members of the local party association who took a rather less utilitarian view when it came to the proper relationship between sinners and forgiveness.

It's perhaps rather less easy to find an uplifting moral in the case of Neil Hamilton, the boy from the mining village of Fleur-de-Lys in Monmouthshire, who had the distinction of getting into a truth-telling contest with Mohamed Al Fayed, and losing. Hamilton said that the old Egyptian fantasist was lying when he claimed that he, Hamilton, had received thousands of pounds in cash, handed to him in brown envelopes in return for various political favours, including asking questions in the Commons.

Hamilton (Amman Valley Grammar School and the University College of Wales, Aberystwyth) had been corporate affairs minister when he was forced to resign in 1994 to bring his action against the owner of Harrod's, a man who at one stage said he understood you hired MPs as you would hail taxis in the street. In the end, years later, a libel jury didn't believe Hamilton, who nevertheless went on denying that he took the money. In the dear innocent days of not so long ago many of us would have found Al Fayed's story incredible. But now we knew such things could happen, and had happened.

They'd happened, for example, to Tim Smith, who had been a junior minister in the Northern Ireland Office and MP for Beaconsfield. Smith admitted taking up to £25,000 in cash from Al Fayed. As a consequence he resigned and, at the time of Hamilton's libel action, was the subject of a rather poignant footnote in the *Guardian*. "Mr. Smith is understood to be working as a chartered accountant in Devon." Oh, the cruel vagueness of that 'understood' for a once successful and ambitious man.

In the case of Neil Hamilton, though, it seems to me that, even if he had been able to demonstrate beyond question that the brown envelope allegations against him were entirely without foundation, it wouldn't have saved him from the wreckage of his career or made much difference to the public's view of him. Like Rod Richards, he was to some extent condemned by what he hadn't done or, more accurately, what he had done but which wasn't against the rules.

Among the various methods by which he sought to have a good time at a low cost, there was his trip to the Ritz Hotel in Paris in 1987 as the guest of its owner, yes, Mohamed Al Fayed. The cost of Hamilton's stay there was put at around £6,000 when calculated in the light of prices at the time of his libel trial. In court he admitted that he had a sense of shame about his indulgence. He and his wife, the formidable Christine, drank vintage champagne every night and in other ways enjoyed the hotel's kitchens and cellars.

Any of us might have done the same, I suppose, but in one regard in particular the Hamiltons betrayed their character. They agreed they had made full use of the minibar in their room. But like everyone else in the world Neil Hamilton must realise that using a hotel minibar is the most expensive way known to man of getting a drink. Someone who does so with such abandon is clearly unfit to hold office in an economic ministry. If lack of style were a crime, the smartest lawyers in the world couldn't have kept him out of gaol.

It seems to me too that there is something distinctively Welsh about Hamilton's story. His chippiness, his self-satisfaction, and his capacity for freeloading are particularly reminiscent of the way in which councillors in South Wales used to conduct themselves. Maybe it was in the air of the places in which he lived as a child and as a young man, something you could *catch*.

But it's also a very modern affair. The voters of Tatton, his Cheshire constituency, condemned Hamilton, which was as it should have been. At the same time there emerged a curious belief that it is possible to draw up rules which will compel people to be honest and which will force them to adhere to standards of probity and openness beyond the reach of most people in whom a pulse is still detectable. The difficulty we face is in drawing a distinction between a necessary rigour in the conduct of public affairs and the excesses of the new puritanism. The test should be, I suppose, whether an MP or an assembly member or a councillor is influenced to do something he would not otherwise have done.

When it comes to the tricky questions thus raised, many of us turn to the case of David Lloyd George, by common consent one of the great Prime Ministers of the twentieth century, but also a compulsive adulterer, probably a perjurer and certainly a man who was none too scrupulous when it came to trying to make some cash. For example, the affair of Keith Best and the British Telecom shares looks like a man trying to rob his own piggy bank with a kitchen knife when you put it alongside Lloyd George and the Marconi company.

In 1912, Marconi signed a contract to establish six wireless telegraphy stations around the world at a cost of £60,000 each. We should bear in mind that that's something like £3,500,000 at modern prices. No sooner had the scheme become public than there were rumours that members of the government had acted improperly. Shortly before the flotation of the British Marconi company, the Attorney General, Sir Rufus Isaacs, bought ten thousand shares. Isaacs' brother, as it happened, was a director. He bought the shares for two pounds each but, when they went public, they sold at four pounds. Lloyd George, who was Chancellor of the Exchequer, bought two thousand pounds' worth. (The equivalent of £120,000 in the year 2000.)

When the story emerged a House of Commons select committee was set up to investigate it. The committee divided along party lines and a minority report accused Lloyd George and Isaacs of 'grave impropriety'. At the end of the two-day debate that followed the report, the Government used its majority to see that there were no consequences for the men who were, after all, two of its most senior members. Indeed, so unconcerned were they that four months later Isaacs was made Lord Chancellor and so head of the entire legal system. As such, one of his responsibilities was to see to it that other people didn't do what he clearly had done.

To look at these events with a modern eye is to be astounded, and while some people obviously had serious misgivings, it's clear that such matters were viewed rather differently in another political age. Even Lloyd George, though, took a huge risk when (like Bevan, Phillips and Crossman years later) he sued a newspaper for libel, despite the fact that it seems probable its allegations were true.

In 1909 the *People* newspaper carried a series of articles in which it was hinted that Lloyd George had been about to be cited in a divorce case, but that the would-be plaintiff had been bought off for £20,000 (more than £1 million in modern terms). The problem he faced was not the same as would have confronted a modern politician. As John Grigg points out in his biography of Lloyd George, "According to the standards of

Victorian and Edwardian England, the only breach of sexual morality that a public man had to avoid, if he wished to stay in public life, was any that had the effect of breaking his own, or someone else's marriage. Fornication and adultery were not, in themselves, a threat to his career."

L.G. went to court. What was decisive in the action was not so much what he said as what someone else did.

His wife, Margaret, spent her time in North Wales but she could hardly have been unaware of L.G.'s notorious womanising. Years before he had, in effect, warned her that it would happen if she didn't join him in London. In this case Maggie, as he called her, did what other politicians' wives have done in the years since. Like, for example, Hillary Clinton (although in the First Lady's case, ineffectively), she publicly proclaimed her belief in her husband's innocence. Margaret Lloyd George didn't have to say anything. Her simple presence in court as she listened to her husband's protestations of innocence was enough to intimidate the defence. Edward Carson, the formidable barrister and Ulster politician who had been Oscar Wilde's nemesis, apologised to the court on behalf of his clients, who agreed to pay Lloyd George a thousand pounds in damages.

That money, by the way, was eventually used to build a village hall in Llanystumdwy. As it happened, in the previous year Lloyd George had been paid three hundred guineas in settlement of a libel action against the *Bystander* magazine, again over allegations of sexual misconduct. That money had gone to Caernarfon cottage hospital. It's easy to imagine good causes all over North Wales competing furiously to be the beneficiaries of the next adultery Lloyd George did not commit.

Throughout his life it's clear that Lloyd George suffered from that disease to which American presidents, notably Kennedy and Clinton in recent years, were particularly susceptible. He was incapable of keeping his hands off the many girls by whom he was surrounded and who were dazzled at being so close to the centre of power.

"My mother had to console people to whom he had made an advance. But these were people who had said 'no' and had been accepted. But they were unhappy, they were distressed, about having advances made to them. She did, I think, tell L.G. that this was not acceptable behaviour, but I don't think he took any notice."

That was the account given by Jennifer, the daughter of Frances Stevenson, who had long been Lloyd George's mistress. Margaret Lloyd George, by then Dame Margaret, died in 1941. In 1943, at the age of eighty, he married Frances, who later became the first Countess Lloyd-George of Dwyfor. But one puzzle remains to this day: was Lloyd George Jennifer's father? The answer is he probably was, although not definitely. For a substantial part of his life Lloyd George maintained two homes. One in Surrey, which he shared with Frances, and the other in North Wales where his wife and children had remained during his long political career. When Jennifer was born, a coded telegram was send to L.G. who was on holiday with his family in Llanystumdwy: "The parcel we were expecting has arrived."

What is most extraordinary about these events from today's perspective is not simply that the people involved were prepared to accept them, however reluctantly, but that not a word about this arrangement was ever printed in the newspapers. It might have been long after L.G.'s days as Prime Minister, but at a time when he still had big political ambitions. As for Jennifer herself, who was never told definitively who her father was, she explained the manners of the day: "People didn't go around in those days putting two and two together. They didn't ask."

All this is of course a long time ago. Lloyd George died in 1945 and lived through an era in which there was far less exposure of the private lives of public people. Not that it didn't exist at all, as he discovered himself, and not that he didn't have to take some extraordinary risks to save his career. But, as John Grigg said, big personalities tend to have big flaws.

Is that an excuse, though? That you can't have one without the other? It's undeniable that much of Lloyd George's behaviour was entirely reprehensible, and there are plenty more examples of misconduct in his life other than those I've outlined here – the sale of honours, for instance. If he had lived in an age of institutionalised sanctimony policed by long lenses, listening devices and kiss 'n' tell, it seems unlikely that he could have survived as a politician. No-one, not even addicts of virtual history, can say what the exact consequences of that would have been, but it seems certain we would have been deprived of an exceptional talent. The same might have been true of many others whose weaknesses would earn them thunderous condemnation in the twenty-first century tabloids. Churchill's financial arrangements come to mind in this context, as does Hugh Gaitskell's womanising.

That may be one reason why exceptional talents are less and less attracted by political life. From membership of the National Assembly for Wales to the presidency of the United States, the first qualification for office seems to be a clean record, financial rigour, a lack of passion, an absence of idiosyncrasy of any kind and a mind-numbing capacity for providing a politically correct response in any given circumstances. Either that or, as in the case of President Clinton, a highly-developed ability to dissemble. Even in Clinton's case that didn't keep him out of difficulties for ever, but his continuing popularity perhaps indicated that the public are less obsessed with so-called moral issues than they are given credit for.

In the scandals that have struck Welsh politicians there seems to have been a substantial element of rough justice. Most of them have paid deserved penalties of one kind or another. The only person who has undermined Rod Richards's career is Rod Richards. But their cases have frequently given rise to demands for stricter regulation so that, for example, Elin Jones, the Plaid Cymru assembly member for Ceredigion, feels obliged to declare "occasional singing and composing" in the register of members' interests. Christine Gwyther included: "Dinner for Member and Spouse – Early Potato Conference in Pembrokeshire, May 1999".

We shouldn't laugh but it's impossible not to. Who thinks that politicians will start writing down the things that really matter to them – mistresses, habitual drunkenness, taking bribes, hanging round public lavatories and the like – in among the endless lists of trivia compiled by their less colourful colleagues? Who thinks we are better governed because of a public display of virtue by those doing the governing? How long has demonstrable dullness been the chief qualification for soliciting votes? Who wonders now if, as we wade about up to our armpits in probity, a new Lloyd George isn't deciding to become a rock singer instead?

6. Redwood Gets Romantic

For many of those whose long-cherished dream it had been, the arrival of the elected Welsh assembly turned out to be rather like a coveted Christmas present which had been despatched without instructions or batteries. Those who had opposed its creation, like the Conservatives, jeered at the general uselessness of the treasured gift although they couldn't resist trying to play with it themselves. Others looked enviously at their cousins in Scotland who'd been given a more powerful model, with flashy law-making powers and a tax-raising attachment, even if they'd promised faithfully they wouldn't actually use the latter because it was so dangerous.

The truth of the matter was that the new constitutional system was an explosive mixture of the cynical and the incoherent. Wales, a very coy mistress, was wooed with honeyed words that promised undying democracy. Transparency, openness, inclusivity, devo-lovers whispered lubriciously in the ears of a fretful virgin, who forgot a mother's warning that politicians were only ever after one thing. Secondary legislation, they murmured in a torrent of erotic language. A bonfire of the quangos, they promised recklessly, knowing how to insinuate their way into a girl's secret, passionate dreams. It was enough – just – to get her into bed. But, came the dawn...

As the mists of romance cleared slowly, the true nature of the national assembly revealed itself, although it took many of its members a long time to understand it. Some, indeed, preferred not to make the effort. Essentially the deal was this: from July 1999, when the necessary powers were transferred, sixty elected people would perform in public many of the duties previously carried out in private by three Welsh Office ministers. They would administer Wales but they would not run it. In theory they had immense powers, particularly because they were in charge of spending £8 billion a year. They were not, however, given any responsibility for raising this money. So, for example, it was open to them to take a few million pounds out of the health service budget and spend it on schools instead; or take money from education and build roads with it. Naturally they were never going to do any such thing because the voters would never tolerate cuts in spending on health and education; in particular they would never put up with the idea that people in Wales were for some reason getting inferior services to those enjoyed by people in England.

In addition to things they could do but wouldn't, there were any number of things assembly members thought they could do but weren't able to after all. Introducing a calf disposal scheme, rejecting performance-related pay for teachers, making Wales a GM-free zone were among them. The power always lay somewhere else, in Westminster perhaps, or in Europe; sometimes no-one seemed exactly sure where specific authority might be found.

Then there were things they might have done but didn't. For example, when invited to take part (in a spirit of inclusivity, natch) in an examination of some of the problems of the health service, Plaid Cymru said there was no point since everyone knew what the problems were – too few staff and not enough money – so there was no point in having meetings about it. From Plaid Cymru's point of view non-involvement also had the advantage of ensuring that the party would be able to avoid the blame for anything, always the first instinct of the true political mind.

There were also things they thought they might have done but someone else did for them. When it came to a £25 million grant to the British Aerospace factory on Deeside, it was Rhodri Morgan, as both First Secretary and Economic Development Secretary, who took the decision to refuse it. He was acting perfectly properly on the advice of the Welsh Industrial Development Advisory Board, but not only did he do so in private but no-one was allowed to know what explanation lay behind his refusal because the company itself, for commercial reasons, had asked that the background to his judgement should remain secret.

At the same time no-one seemed to have brought the matches necessary to start the bonfire of the quangos, a process promised by Ron Davies in those gung-ho days when he was trying to get people to vote for an assembly. It was true that the

Welsh Development Agency, the Development Board for Rural Wales and the Land Authority for Wales were all rolled into one super quango, but that had been done by Ron, unaided, as Secretary of State, in the days when the assembly was no more than a speculative twinkle in his eye. It was also the case that the Cardiff Bay Development Corporation was wound up a little earlier than had been originally intended, but Ron decided that by himself as well.

There were also things they could do and did, including restoring free eye tests for some groups of people, although civil servants said this was probably a waste of money, and debating and agreeing regulations on matters like home improvement grants. Frankly, there's not a lot of fun in that or in the many other similar issues with which they were presented. They could also get rid of Alun Michael as First Secretary which, in the event, because they could, they did.

The truth of the matter is that when it came to devolution the prime rule of government asserted itself: that is to do as little as you can get away with. The particular strategy for Wales was to adopt a method which would allow the government to tell opponents that it wasn't doing anything very much, just letting a chink of democratic light fall into the corners of a devolved system that already existed, but at the same time reassure devolutionists that here was a genuine advance in self-determination. It was, as usual, neither.

Innocent people, among whom I number myself, wondered where the Welsh plan fitted into the new constitutional arrangements which were apparently a crucial aspect of the way in which New Labour was transforming old Britain. It was a question I put to quite a lot of politicians in the course of researching this book. Was there, somewhere in Downing Street, a master plan which made sense of the changes being introduced so rapidly? Devolution for Scotland and Wales; restoration of devolved government in Northern Ireland; forms of proportional representation for some elections; elected mayors, in particular one in London; reform of the House of Lords. What was the big idea that lay behind them all?

A couple of people who usually have answers for pretty well everything had ready explanations, although the fact that they were different explanations does give some pause for thought. For example, Rhodri Morgan said there was no master plan but he nevertheless believed that between them the various changes could lead to only one conclusion.

"It does make you think that in ten years' time people will say its about time we sorted this lot out with a written constitution. I think a momentum will develop whereby we have a written constitution in the next ten years. The snowball is half way down the hill now and it's gathered a lot of momentum."

For his part, Peter Hain had a predictably Peter Hain-like analysis. "There's a common theme to it which, from my point of view, is that socialism is about decentralising power, spreading power, or it's about nothing. From that point of view it is a very coherent package. You don't have to be a signed-up socialist, though, to believe that the best way of running a country is by getting decisions, appropriate decisions, closer to the level at which they are most appropriate to be taken."

At this point my notes say: "Little history lecture here", but later he went on... "I actually think that in fifty years' time the nation state as a political unit will be less significant politically because of, on the one hand, the European level, and on the other hand the level of Scotland, Wales and the regions of England because that is the way economics and production systems are going. That also makes a lot of sense in terms of where power is really exercised."

Well, absorbing though all this is, both the ten year view and the fifty year view, I have to say that everyone else to whom I addressed this question felt that there was no master plan of any kind, no big idea. Rather they believed that Tony Blair's strategy was to shoot first and ask questions afterwards. He clearly does not know, for instance, what will eventually become of the partially-reformed House of Lords, but it was also obvious that if some start on change wasn't made in a hurry then nothing at all would happen. That was the lesson of previous attempts at reform. In the same way, if the government hadn't raced ahead with the referendum on Welsh devolution within a matter of a few months of being elected, it would probably have been bogged down in argument for another ten or twenty years. It only happened at all because it happened fast.

But the fact that the series of constitutional changes introduced at such speed had no coherent structure, the fact that it was impossible to see how one part of the process related to all the others in a United Kingdom context, had two important consequences. One was that it seemed inevitable that it wouldn't stop there. In the Welsh assembly the carpet-chewing frustration induced in members by the way in which the system seemed to thwart even their most humble ambitions led to thoughts of greater power. It was noticeable, for example, that when, at the Labour Party conference in September 1999, Paul Murphy, as Secretary of State, pronounced Welsh devolution to be a settled question, there was no answering chorus of assent, even within his own party.

The instability that people now discern in the constitutional organisation of the United Kingdom, with an independent Scotland forecast either with fear or relish most days of the week, has driven many people to an orgy of sentimentalism very thinly disguised as political thought. What is happening, they argue, is nothing less than the end of Britain, although some of those who say this sort of thing, and who should know better, have an uncertain grasp of what and where Britain actually is, and of its history.

There is, for example, a geographical term, the British Isles, but the island which contains Ireland has never been described by the adjective British. The Kingdom of Great Britain, comprising England, Scotland and Wales, came into being only in 1707 with the Act of Union between England and Scotland, although the two countries had been united under a single monarch since 1603. Wales was united with England under the two Acts of Union of 1536 and 1543 although that arrangement was imposed by Henry VIII rather than agreed by two separate, sovereign, parliaments – chiefly because Wales didn't actually have one. The United Kingdom currently consists of Great Britain (England, Scotland and Wales) and Northern Ireland. From 1801 until 1922 the United Kingdom comprised England, Scotland, Wales and Ireland, but that description ceased with the establishment of the Irish Free State. It was at that time, of course, that a devolved system of government was introduced for Northern Ireland, something all governments in recent years have desperately tried to maintain or restore. It's interesting that the Conservative Party managed at the same time to warn of the grave dangers of any similar arrangement for, say, Scotland and/or Wales.

That's quite enough of that, but it does give an indication of how complex a question this is and how people may well mean different things when they talk of Britain and British. Many simply see those terms as interchangeable with England and English. But then, someone like my own father began life, in 1903, as a British subject but not, since he was born in Co. Sligo, a resident of Britain. In 1922, with the establishment of the Free State, he became an Irish citizen, although he lived most of the rest of his life in Wales. During that period he saw his country's official name change from Irish Free State to Eire to Ireland. The questions this raised obviously filtered in some way into my own life. I can remember asking him – and I must have been very young, certainly under nine years old – whether we were British. It was perhaps easiest for him to answer, as he did, 'Yes', because I was, he wasn't then, although he had been once.

In these circumstances it's not surprising that some people get confused. So it was that John Major, opposing devolution, warned of the end of a thousand years of British history, although there had been no such thing. Mr. Major, famously, was educationally deprived, but John Redwood, as a Fellow of All Souls, the eggheads' college, really ought to have known better. Nevertheless he was capable of writing: "The United Kingdom has been a most successful country. Following English and Welsh Union in 1485 and full Scottish union in 1707, there has been a great flourishing of technical, cultural and economic achievement by the British people."

Apart from the obvious non sequitur contained in that argument, Redwood doesn't even know the dates of the Acts of Union of England and Wales, confusing them with the accession of Henry Tudor who was to some extent Welsh. I suppose it's only charitable to put this lapse down to the passion which seized him as he sat down to write his book, *The Death of Britain?*, complete with enigmatic question mark. Sacked by William Hague for being too chilling a presence in the shadow cabinet, he turned out to be an incorrigible romantic, brimming over with sceptred isle prose. He wrote of the threat of globalisation: "...an even more rapid technical revolution is being hurled against Dover's cliffs", and flourished portentous inversions such as: "The Royal Yacht *Britannia* is part of the Navy Royal".

He was particularly fascinating when he turned the full power of his intellect on what he saw as the contradictions involved in reform of the House of Lords. In that, he argued, Labour were opposed to the hereditary principle but went on: "Labour clearly support the hereditary principle when it comes to the rest of us. There is no statement in the Labour manifesto that inheritance in property, shares, land, buildings or businesses is against the public interest or should be stopped."

Does he really not get it, you wonder. Does he genuinely think that the power, however meagre it has become, granted in perpetuity by accident of birth to a small number of people to have a special place in the legislative process, in other words to tell the rest of us what to do, in however circumscribed a way, does he really believe that this is the equivalent of inheriting your parents' suburban semi? Or is this simply a form of Vulcan humour for which our unsophisticated world is not yet ready?

There were many more barmy ramblings of this nature as Redwood meandered through the terrors of the new Britain he apparently believed was almost upon us. For example, he trembled in fearful anticipation when he contemplated the abolition of the monarchy, with the Queen and her successors being replaced as head of state by the Prime Minister. No, I don't know who's proposed this either.

"In circumstances where a Prime Minister had a narrow majority in the House of Commons, he would have to come back and vote during the course of an evening even if there were a state banquet taking place. At the moment it is possible to finesse this with foreign visitors as the Queen and other members of the royal family are present as principal hostess and hosts for the occasion. The Prime Minister can slip out to do his duty. It would be more difficult if he were the host."

You might think that a government which could change the system sufficiently to get rid of the monarchy might also manage to make a few other necessary adjustments to allow the Prime Minister to finish his dinner with dignity on particularly important occasions. Or perhaps get a president. But if you thought that you would evidently not have the keen analytical mind of a John Redwood.

Other books with apocalyptic titles piled up in the shops with authors wailing loudly as they cursed the folly that had brought brave old Britain to its deathbed. No-one laid about him with more fervour than Peter Hitchens, to whom devolution was just another symptom in a decline which had begun with the Lady Chatterley obscenity trial in 1960 and culminated in the premiership of Tony Blair. According to Hitchens' book *The Abolition of Britain*, virtually every innovation since that time had made things worse including (honestly) central heating.

"The spread of central heating and double glazing has allowed even close-knit families to avoid each other's company in well-warmed houses, rather than huddling round a simple hearth forced into unwanted companionship, and so compelled to adapt to each other's foibles and become more social, less selfish beings."

Please, tell me it's a satire.

There were plenty of other similar ravings from people who, until then, had thought that Britain was England and didn't take kindly to the suggestion that there might be a bit more to it than that. The truth is that this obsessive and inaccurate sentimentality has become little more than a coded attack on change, a plea not to meddle with a system which has served us happily from as far back in the mists of time as, well, 1922. It serves the same symbolic purpose as the Pound does in the sloganising of Eurosceptics: something that unarguably represents the total brilliance of our own heritage as compared with the inadequacy of what the Frogs, Wops, Huns and the rest of them foolishly imagine to be real currencies. In such conflicts of opinion, rational argument is often the first casualty.

Even a passing acquaintanceship with the history of the various constituent parts that make up, or from time to time have made up, the United Kingdom allows you to recognise the fluidity of the concept of being British and the way in which the relationships between those parts have been revised and adjusted in one way or another down to the present day. It has not always been comfortable, as the Irish example demonstrates only too clearly, nor, as we can see from the same instance, has it necessarily been conclusive, but it does demonstrate the problems of confusing geography with politics.

Wales is self-evidently a word describing an identifiable part of the United Kingdom, but what it is to be Welsh (or Scottish or Irish, come to that) is much more difficult to interpret. It is not only in many ways a subjective matter in which people define their particular understanding of their own Welshness, but it clearly changes with time and events. Not all that long ago, for example, to write the word 'Welsh' rather than 'British' in the nationality column of hotel registers might have been seen as provocatively nationalistic. Now it seems to me, from unscientific observation, to be commonplace. I can only cite as evidence the fact that I've made the change myself, that political and constitutional adjustments have invested the description with much greater meaning.

Even within Wales, though, a definition of what it is to be Welsh can be difficult to pin down. For example, there are many people who do not speak the Welsh language who believe they are not regarded as properly Welsh by those who do. There is a continuing tension in this issue. That is because for some, language is not simply one, optional, mark of nationality, but the essence of it. In recent years some of the heat has gone out of this argument, although the fire is by no means extinguished. It's also the case that there is an interdependence between the two linguistic communities which often goes unremarked. It is rarely mentioned that some of the most important ways in which Welsh is sustained exist only thanks to the goodwill of those who do not speak it. The Welsh television channel, S4C, for example, is funded at least in part by taxpayers in England. Perhaps that's one of the things they mean by inclusivity.

Then again, it seems to be significant that there is now in existence something called the Welsh Conservative Party. When that style was proposed in the seventies, red-faced unionists denounced the idea that it should adopt any form of words which might be seen as officially acknowledging that Wales was in some way not the same as England – in effect suggesting that

England-and-Wales was not one, indivisible place. But the Conservatives are realists and they're quite happy to give themselves any title which might help in the vote-gathering department.

Another straw in the wind can be seen in the way in which Labour politicians have adopted Owain Glyndwr as some kind of patron saint. The point about Glyndwr, long treated as the private property of Plaid Cymru, is his status as a man who is portrayed as taking up arms against England in the cause of an independent Wales and who briefly held Wales's first parliaments at the beginning of the fifteenth century. Despite the fact that he might be held to be a proto-nationalist, these days Rhodri Morgan speaks of him in admiring terms and Alun Michael, as I've mentioned, claimed that Glyndwr would have agreed with him on the question of Objective One match funding.

It is perhaps the fluid nature of our individual ideas of nationality that has led Plaid Cymru apparently to deny its own first principles when it comes to its ultimate objective. To accuse the party of being in favour of independence for Wales is to provoke furious denials. As we know, during the assembly election campaign of 1999 its leaders behaved as if, by making this suggestion, the newspapers had published paparazzi pictures of them furtively indulging in some particularly shameful vice.

Only people whose sense of the absurd had been surgically removed could have failed to enjoy this argument. Plaid Cymru was trying to deny what was clearly the case, that the party was in favour of Welsh independence, while Labour and the Liberal Democrats were pretending that Plaid was trying to keep its true beliefs a secret. It all turned, not on philosophy and the core beliefs of the party, but on the use and meaning of a particular word. Gwynfor Evans, born in 1912, and so rather older than the party itself, produced the evidence of his long period in office. "Never in thirty-six years as president did I advocate independence for Wales."

Others suggested they'd virtually never heard of the word until it had been flourished at them by political opponents. Inquirers were directed to the writings of Saunders Lewis, playwright, arsonist and troublemaker, who had been one of the founders of Plaid Cymru in 1925. The casuistic style of argument favoured by Lewis's adopted Catholic faith showed very clearly when he addressed this matter.

"Above all, let us not ask for independence for Wales. Not because it isn't practical but because it isn't worth having... it is a materialist and evil thing, leading to violence and oppression." What he was talking about, he said, was not independence but freedom, and, blow me down, anticipating by more than seventy years the speeches made by Dafydd Wigley, Ieuan Wyn Jones and the rest of them. Lewis looked forward to a new, united Europe... "We who are Welsh claim that we are responsible for the civilisation and the ways of social life in our part of Europe. That is the political ambition of the Nationalist Party."

We'll leave aside the fact that modern Plaid Cymru parts company with old Saunders when it comes to the term nationalist, once a badge of honour, now denounced as a crude slur employed by the party's opponents. We'll listen instead to the echoes of his aspirations contained in a speech in April 1999 by Cynog Dafis, a member of the national assembly and at that time also the MP for Ceredigion. Cynog said that over the next fifteen years the status of Wales would rise and he went on: "Our representation will be perhaps through a Britannic confederation or through the European union... We see ourselves maximising our self-government in Europe, having a voice in the EU."

Did that man say self-government? Yes he did but, according to this particular form of English, self-government doesn't mean independence. Nor does dominion status, favoured by Saunders Lewis, or home rule or self-determination or full national status or even, as was once adopted as the official objective of Plaid Cymru, socialist republicanism. The new man at the top of Plaid Cymru, Ieuan Wyn Jones, stretched language even further when he was campaigning for the party's presidency in July 2000. He too talked about 'full national status', and specifically said that Wales should have the same status as, for example, Denmark or Ireland. At the same time, he maintained, this did not mean independence. Do they say that, I wonder, in Copenhagen or in Dublin?

At this stage you might ask why, if they don't have anything more intelligent to say, people bother saying anything at all. But on reflection you realise that this way of describing the world fits very neatly into the whole devolution process in which language is carefully used to reassure the voters rather than to alarm them. It suits the party to suggest to people that not only doesn't Plaid Cymru seem to have the courage of its convictions but that it doesn't actually have any convictions to have the courage of. You can vote for us, the message is, in the certain knowledge that nothing terrible will happen. Nationalists? Who? Us? Independence? Never heard of it. We are safe, we are solid. Above all, we are respectable.

To some extent this might be seen as a recognition of the fact that it's out of tune with our times to talk about great political projects. In much of the world what was the twentieth century's great contest between capitalism and public ownership has ended in a draw. In the United Kingdom private enterprise in business co-exists peacefully with a decent, although by no means lavish, welfare state. In its turn that implies certain levels of taxation to meet public expenditure and, despite what the Tories say from time to time, it seems unlikely that any party is going to alter that level in any significant way, particularly while we enjoy a period of comparative economic prosperity.

In these circumstances it's almost certainly a waste of time – counter-productive, even – for Plaid Cymru to start banging on about independence, an idea which has both a revolutionary flavour and a clarity of expression with which most voters seem to be out of sympathy. If big ideas of this kind are unpopular, then how much better it is to be a party almost indistinguishable from any other. So instead of talking about constitutional objectives it's perhaps more convenient to lurk behind low-level linguistic conjuring tricks ("There's no such thing as independence in the modern world, we are all inter-dependent..." etc.), or go on about the uncertainty of the structures that will result from the enlargement and development of the European Union and so forth. Anything, in other words, rather than answer the question.

Above all, though, this is a recognition of the two-part structure that has now come to Welsh politics. Such indications as there are suggest that, at a general election, old voting patterns are likely to reassert themselves and the Plaid Cymru support will revert to its previous ten per cent plus-or-minus levels. In that UK context the independence question might be of greater significance. But what's most important to Plaid Cymru is to build its support in the assembly, not by bothering the electorate with troublesome notions of self-government, but by explaining how brilliant Plaid politicians can run Wales better than the familiar Labour dead-beats. On this basis independence, or whatever you call it, although not an irrelevant question in the Plaid Cymru scheme of things, is one best left for the future. The momentum created by the assembly is clearly a tentative step towards further self-determination for Wales; it's just that some people prefer not to talk about what it really means at the moment.

In its turn that suggests everyone else might have to start addressing it sooner rather than later. Within months of the assembly members taking their seats, the summary dismissal of Alun Michael showed us that, while the most important arguments ostensibly take place between the parties in Crickhowell House, they will in reality be between Cardiff and London. Events began badly enough, but it's not difficult to imagine how much worse they might be in the event, say, of a Labour administration in the assembly and a Conservative government in Westminster. Or with a Plaid Cymru administration in Wales and *either* a Labour or Conservative government at the other end of the M4.

Among the many tortured recriminations in his book, John Redwood includes this: "Nationalist movements in both Scotland and Wales will now have an easy time creating campaigns against the power of the centre". In this at least Redwood is clearly correct. It's already started. But the point is that this will not be the preserve simply of nationalists. Every politician looking for someone to blame will insist it's all London's fault. During the Objective One debates even the Conservatives fell in behind the demand from Plaid Cymru and the Liberal Democrats (not to mention the unspoken desires of Labour) that the government should hand over its share of the cash at once, and in full. We all know that Conservatives, like all politicians, are capable of saying exactly the opposite when their own party is in power, but if they did so to suit the convenience of their own regime, the moral force of their argument would be pretty well eradicated.

There are, too, less materialistic disputes to be had. For example, it would be a simple matter to frame Westminster legislation to allow the Welsh assembly to make a decision on whether or not to ban fox-hunting. Of course they'd ban it anyway because that's the sort of people they are, but if devolution means anything why should assembly members be deprived of the moral warmth of doing it themselves? Labour members of the assembly didn't want to take the decision on fox-hunting, but that's no reason why they should not have been obliged to do so. They wanted responsibility, now they ought to take it. Or again, if Welsh people were for a long time considered to be socially responsible enough (and sufficiently different from the English) to be able to decide for themselves whether pubs should open or close on a Sunday, why can't they maintain or abolish Clause 28 of the Local Government Act which prohibits the 'promotion' of homosexuality in schools? They are free to do that in Scotland, just as they are allowed to abolish tuition fees for university students. There doesn't seem to be any particular reason why the Welsh assembly shouldn't spend part of its education budget on the same measure if it wants to.

What is important about these questions is not whether people should or should not ban fox-hunting, repeal Clause 28 or abolish tuition fees. It's a matter of who, under the new dispensation, should be allowed to make these decisions. The fact is that, for the first time in history, Welsh politicians share something with each other from which their colleagues outside are excluded: the need to assert their own authority. Welsh devolution is not in itself a big idea. Nevertheless it marks the beginning of a new way of looking at the world – something of which no-one can see the ultimate consequences.

7. Prince Charles Has A Word With God

The clearest indication that there was no carefully thought-out constitutional blueprint in Downing Street or anywhere else when Tony Blair took office was contained in the government's plans for the future of the royal family. None. No plans, that is, rather than no future, although if the process of change had any internal coherence it could hardly have left them out. That is particularly the case because of the thunderous way in which Blair has subsequently denounced the hereditary principle as applied to the House of Lords. After all, if it's wrong for the Earl of This or the Marquis of That to assume powers (however minor) over the rest of us because of some service to the Crown in, say, the seventeenth century, it inescapably means that the monarchy itself, the apex of such privilege, should be subject to the same objections.

The simple explanation for this omission is that Tories in the House of Lords over the years frequently prevented Labour governments from doing what they wanted to do while the monarchy did not. It was therefore more a question of political convenience than of principle. So much so that a number of hereditary peers have been allowed to remain in the Lords until the full process of reform can be carried out. Will that task ever be completed, many people ask, or will the Lords remain for ever a teeny-weeny bit pregnant, as it were, in the constitutional scheme of things?

That could well happen, particularly as there are plenty of anomalies in that part of the system, the life peerage, which is supposed to be more in tune with the democratic principles of a modern state. There is, for example, the case of Lord Kagan who came to prominence as the manufacturer of the Gannex mack, a garment made famous by Harold Wilson when he was Prime Minister during the 1960s. Joe Kagan was knighted for his services to something or other and later made a life peer. There came a time, though, when he was sent to prison for financial offences and, as has happened to other people in these circumstances, he was stripped of his knighthood. Nevertheless, until the day he died he was entitled to go on sitting in the Lords, voting on this Bill and that, a privilege denied the rest of us, and no-one could do anything about it.

Such cases are often used in support of the argument that, since pretty awful people advance in the world without the benefit of hereditary connections, there's no need to be quite so sniffy about those who enjoy the advantages of a leg-up from a prudent ancestor. Someone, for instance, who, in the 1920s, forked out £50,000 (a vast sum in today's money) to buy a barony under the useful money-making scheme established by Lloyd George. Such people, it's argued, bring experience and knowledge which would not otherwise be at the service of the nation. (Quite why not, I can't say.)

It's for such reasons that you could understand why, when the reform was reaching its final stages in the Lords, it upset someone called the Earl of Burford. Now, although an earl, young Burford was not actually a member of the House of Lords. However, as the eldest son of the Duke of St. Albans (who is hereditary falconer to the Queen and a descendant of Charles II's most famous mistress, Nell Gwynn), he was entitled to sit on the steps of the throne in the Lords. Because of this he was able to make his noisy protests heard when, finally, New Labour took an axe to this silken line of tradition stretching back three centuries and more. His opinion was that the changes being made to the Upper House were all part of a Brussels conspiracy. He perhaps didn't realise that he was making the government's point for them, but he would have been exceptionally bright, for your average aristocrat, if he had done so.

It also turns out that in this world even the definition of heredity has its flexible aspects. Geoffrey Russell, 4th Baron Ampthill, was allowed to sit in the Lords even though his mother was technically a virgin at the time of his birth. In a divorce case in 1923, the 3rd Lord Ampthill claimed that his wife, Christabel, had committed adultery and that Geoffrey was the result of that liaison. Christabel agreed that no "normal" sexual intercourse had taken place between her and her husband, but she insisted that the baby was the result of sharing a bed with Lord Ampthill during which "Hunnish scenes" (Don't ask.) had taken place. In 1976 this was good enough for the Committee for Privileges and Geoffrey took his place in the legislature.

Of course it's easy enough to mock the House of Lords, the absurdity of some of the people in it and the methods by which they got there. But just because it's easy doesn't mean we shouldn't do it. What is curious, though, is the reluctance most people have when it comes to subjecting the monarchy to the same sort of scrutiny. When people talked of the need for devolution, their central argument often concerned the desirability of an extension of democracy, but not a single question was asked in formal political debate about the undemocratic monument that is at the centre of our constitution. The truth is it's an awkward issue and we prefer to ignore it, even at times when the occupant of the throne falls to low levels in public esteem. After the abdication of Edward VIII in 1936, for example, a motion in the House of Commons to "remove all monarchical institutions and the hereditary principle" was defeated by 403 votes to five. Despite persistent provocation, especially in the nineteenth century, this is the only time the future of the monarchy has been put to the vote in the Commons.

It seems possible, however, that the present Prince of Wales may turn out to be the man to concentrate minds on the issue once again. He is in one of the unluckiest jobs in the world and, as many of his predecessors have discovered, you can only get it wrong, not least in Wales itself.

Tradition has it that the first prince was presented to the people from the battlements of Caernarfon Castle by his father, Edward I, who had conquered Wales and seen off the last of the country's native princes. He is supposed to have said of the baby, in a piece of thirteenth century spin-doctoring, "Behold, I give you a prince who speaks no English". Most reputable historians insist this is simply a legend, but if it is true it is the first recorded example of the authorities sucking up to the Welsh Language Society.

Unfortunately, the whole Prince of Wales business was immediately off to a bad start. Young Edward, who became Edward II, although being described as "fair of body and great of strength", was the first, but by no means the last, whose downfall was brought about by sex. In his case it was a homosexual liaison with his chum Piers Gaveston. His advancement of this favourite and his refusal to accept Gaveston's exile led to civil war. The prince was declared by Parliament to be "incorrigible without hope of amendment" and was put to death in a gruesome manner at Berkeley Castle. The details need not concern us here; all I'll say is that his execution involved a red hot poker.

Even in the generally disastrous story of princes of Wales this was a spectacularly poor performance, but many others also had a notably hard time of it. The prince who briefly became Edward V, for example, was murdered as a child, one of the Princes in the Tower. Not long after that, Henry VII's son, Arthur, named specifically to conjure up mystical Welsh associations, died young, leaving his title, and his wife, Catherine of Aragon, to his brother, later Henry VIII. Those were the events which were eventually to bring us the Church of England. The man who became Edward VII was Prince of Wales from the time he was one month old until 1901, when he was sixty, and succeeded Queen Victoria. His disreputable behaviour, particularly with women, but in other matters too, was legendary.

In these circumstances even the least superstitious of us might have been inclined to review the whole business of this princedom because of an eerie catalogue of error and misfortune associated with it. Its history suggests it might be useful at least to consult an astrologer before setting up the next one, if such a thing is ever again considered desirable. And that is not least because of the story of the present prince's great-uncle, Edward VIII.

Poor old David, as he was then known, was the first to be shoved through an entirely spurious investiture ceremony at Caernarfon Castle for someone else's political ends – in this instance Lloyd George's, who at the time happened to be Chancellor of the Exchequer and MP for the Caernarfon Boroughs. Edward VIII's story, that of an inadequate man most of whose life consisted largely of self-gratification of one kind or another, is well known. In Wales, of course, he is particularly famous for the occasion when, as King, he turned up at Dowlais during the Depression to pronounce, "Something must be done," and then abdicating before being able to make any contribution to that 'something', whatever it might have been.

The lessons of this unedifying tale, and the life of the man who became the Duke of Windsor, clearly haven't been lost on his great-nephew, Charles, who, despite his tangled love life, is notable above all for his anxious desire to make a contribution, not to be a drone, but instead to be someone who can use his exceptional position to improve the world. And that, in essence, is the trouble.

This state of affairs is of particular interest in Wales because, in modern times at least, it's prompted the royal family, no doubt urged on by governments, to go round trying to make a point about the connection between the title and the place it is supposed to represent. At the end of the 1960s another Caernarfon investiture was considered to be just the thing, particularly in the light of various manifestations of disaffection in Wales – a few bombs, people voting for Plaid Cymru and other outbursts which, particularly in Labour eyes, were considered undesirable. On this occasion the royal family took its reputation for ruthless discipline even further. To prepare for this bogus and embarrassing event Charles was sent to university in Aberystwyth.

It was only for a term, but it would have been a jolt for any upper class twenty-year-old to leave the protective, establishment comforts of Trinity College, Cambridge, for the rougher and less accommodating atmosphere of West Wales. Well, there we are, if you're a prince you've got to do this sort of thing, despite the fact that even the college Principal, Dr. (later Sir) Thomas Parry was among those who didn't really want him there because he wasn't convinced he could guarantee Charles's safety.

Parry had some reason for thinking that. Although it would be an exaggeration to describe Aberystwyth in that period as some kind of hatchet-wielding republican stronghold, a majority of the students would probably have been anti-monarchist, if in a fairly unspecific manner, and virtually all of them would have been, almost by definition, anti-authority. It was also the case that a large number of the students at the college were Welsh-speaking at a time when Welsh language activism was particularly rampant. After all, Aberystwyth was one of the places where they'd practically invented the various language campaigns. To be English in these circumstances, never mind something as provocative as Heir to the Throne, was to be guilty of any number of unspecified crimes.

Despite the unpropitious outlook, though, they more or less got away with it. It was a bit of a circus, but a harmless one on both sides. Charles learned some Welsh (surprisingly well, qualified observers say) and even made a speech in the language to that annual jamboree of Welsh-speaking youth, the Urdd Eisteddfod. Demonstrators demonstrated away from time to time and honour was peacefully satisfied all round. At the same time, however, there's reason to wonder whether Aberystwyth had a deeper effect on Charles's psyche than was generally recognised. Or, perhaps, it was an experience that was to help shape more specifically views he already held.

A quarter of a century later I wrote the script for a BBC film about the events leading up to the investiture. In it, a member of the staff at Pantycelyn Hall, the men's hostel which had been the Prince's home during that period, recalled his reaction when she went to clean his room. He would, she said, stand there with his private detective, bemoaning the injustice of a world in which some cleaned and others were cleaned for. Having got that off his chest he would then go out, taking his anguish with him. Even at the age of twenty he was unmistakably the man we recognise today.

But it was not until much later we were to learn that his time in Aberystwyth perhaps affected his views more than anyone could have expected. At the beginning of the new millennium, documents released from the Public Record Office under the Thirty Year Rule, contained the shattering implication that, in 1969, the Prince of Wales had 'gone native'. That was certainly the view of the then Secretary of State, George Thomas (later Viscount Tonypandy), who used those words in a letter to the Prime Minister, Harold Wilson.

A report in the *Daily Telegraph* on January 1, 2000, said George had claimed that "a dangerous situation" had developed following two speeches by the Prince in which he appeared to endorse the nationalist cause. George, who hated Welsh nationalists even more than he claimed to hate sin, asked for action to curb the Prince's "youthful enthusiasm" and prevent him becoming a pawn of the nationalist movement.

"In my presence in Cardiff," George wrote, "he referred to the 'cultural and political awakening in Wales'. This is *most* useful to the nationalists."

It's tempting to dismiss this as yet another instance of George going round being an old woman, and a virulently anti-nationalist old woman at that. After all, if they hadn't wanted Charles to learn to use phrases like "cultural and political awakening" they shouldn't have sent him to Aberystwyth, where to this day many people still talk of little else, often without any particular evidence of such a thing taking place. But you can see in it, too, early evidence of Charles's weakness for the cultural and spiritual eyewash which has characterised many of the public pronouncements of his maturity. It was perhaps a revealing piece of early evangelism from someone who has become, in various guises, a Man with a Message.

This was evident in his lectures to the nation on the subject of architecture, but was even more pronounced when it came to the matter of GM crops, in particular the views he expressed in the early summer of 2000. His views on genetically modified plants (he calls them genetically *manipulated*, so putting the boot in even by his use of language) were already clear enough, but the reasoning behind them rather less so. Perhaps that was because there wasn't actually any reasoning but, you know, a *feeling*.

This was expressed in a broadcast on Radio 4, designed as a reflection on the series of Reith Lectures which had just concluded. To prepare his mind for this event he had spent some time in a monastery up a mountain somewhere in Greece, reportedly communing with God who, as the Maker of heaven and earth, was obviously the very Chap to consult when making inquiries into the proper working of the crop system.

On this occasion God, as is often the case in the Bible, does not appear to have been terribly specific. Charles's talk reflected this when he suggested that, buried within us all, "there is an instinctive, heartfelt awareness that life provides – if we will allow it to – the most reliable guide as to whether or not our actions are really in the long-term interests of our planet and all the life it supports."

All I can say is that if someone were to try to sell you washing powder on this basis you'd quite rightly turn him away from your door. What did it remind me of? I wondered. Of course, some of the work of the great nature poet, William Wordsworth, and in particular his *Immortality Ode*: "Our birth is but a sleep and a forgetting..." etc. which proposes that human beings carry within them a complete understanding of the natural world but which, beginning with birth itself, is gradually lost as they grow older.

> Shades of the prison-house begin to close
> Upon the growing Boy...

And so on and on.

Would you, I wondered, take a copy of Wordsworth round Tesco's with you as you peered at the labels on the veg? Would you, for that matter, take the Prince of Wales?

This is not to suggest, as some people do, that the Prince is necessarily some kind of crackpot who keeps in touch with nature by holding conversations with geraniums and various other sympathetic plants down at Highgrove. In many ways he reflects the suspicions of the public and the prejudices of the press so that he and the editor of the *Daily Mail* (who makes everyone's flesh creep with talk of "Frankenstein foods") could be one and the same person. But editors do what they have to do to sell newspapers. Perhaps princes, particularly the Heir to the Throne, might need to be more careful.

When it comes down to it, there are only two distinct classes of people in the United Kingdom: the royal family and everyone else. Some problems arise, though, because the royal family itself doesn't appear to understand this distinction. So the persistent collapse of personal relationships is somehow treated as a series of unrelated events instead of what it clearly is, in the jargon of the day, a symptom of a dysfunctional family. The Queen and the Duke of Edinburgh have four children: three of them have been divorced and, in two of those cases, in circumstances that involved considerable public humiliation. The

Queen also has a sister: she is divorced too. The sister is also noted for her insistence on deferential treatment and an indulgent lifestyle clearly verging on the self-destructive.

Faced with this weight of evidence, any other group of people might have looked inwards to reflect on whether there was something in their attitudes, their way of life or their history which might have been the origin of such emotional havoc. Can they communicate with anyone who comes from that part of the territory where other people actually live? They tried Diana, the neurotic, aristocratic, teenage, virgin bride. That was as big a disaster as a Hollywood screenwriter could have devised. Then there was the worldly, rackety, fun-filled Fergie, whose brief career as a royal was almost as catastrophic. It seems likely that Charles's relationship with Camilla Parker Bowles has flourished only because she's been kept at a distance from the Court itself and those who create its peculiarly repressive atmosphere.

Their capacity for self-delusion has been illustrated by no-one more clearly than Prince Edward, the Queen's third son and now the Earl of Wessex. He is apparently trying to make a go of being an ordinary guy. Edward Windsor, the name he's chosen for his adventures in the television trade, runs a production company, Ardent, which among other things, has made a television series on real tennis (derivation, *royal* tennis, brilliant!) which was watched by eight thousand people. Other projects (*Edward on Edward, Castle Ghosts of England*) have been similarly undistinguished according to the critics, of whom there have been a large number. They have also accused him of using his family connections to get the programmes made in the first place.

It would be very surprising if people didn't line up to have a go at Edward because he in the public mind the kind of over-privileged idiot who is bound to make a mess of anything serious. Even so, he revealed his lack of understanding of his own position when, on a visit to the United States in 1999, he answered his detractors by saying, "...they hate anyone who succeeds". In the United States by contrast, he went on, "there is a much greater openness and willingness to take us for what we are. Over there [in England] there's more baggage".

But even in the good old open USA, it appears, what they

take him for is what he is – a prince. I was particularly impressed by the reaction, reported in the *Times*, of Lindy Dekover, an executive vice-president for movies and mini-series at NBC, the sort of title for which the Earl of Wessex would presumably give his right arm. She said: "I can't put my finger on it, but it was kind of awesome".

Many of us know how she felt, but this was just a particularly arresting example of how people at the heart of the royal family believe they can somehow understand the lives of the man and woman in the street. What's more, they are clearly convinced that they know what it's like in the street even though they have never trodden its pavements unaccompanied.

It shows itself in small ways. When the national assembly was to be opened by the Queen, accompanied by the Prince of Wales, in May 1999, objections were raised to the fact that the design of the traditional Royal Standard, the Queen's flag, contained no reference to Wales. It seemed a good idea, therefore, to fly the Prince of Wales's standard alongside it since he'd be there as well. Up at Buckingham Palace officials had to reach for the Valium to counter the effects of such a scandalous suggestion. Didn't people in Wales understand that when the Queen was present *only* the Royal Standard was to be flown. Even so, in a revolutionary gesture to the new institution, the two flags eventually flew side by side. Traditionalists were amazed to discover that the world didn't come to an end after all. It was also particularly pleasing to discover that experts in these matters are known as vexillologists.

The point about protocol is that it is essentially only what happened last time. Public insistence got the flags flown at half mast on Buckingham Palace ("It's never done.") at the time of the death of Princess Diana, when public opinion also forced the Queen to appear on television. But it is only because such things occasionally become matters of open controversy that the rest of us realise how different a world it is that the royal family and their advisers inhabit.

It seems fairly clear, too, that the members of that family themselves aren't aware of the glass screens that are always between them and every other class of person. They have, after all, never lived in any other fashion. So a member of the public couldn't have an everyday, demotic conversation with Prince Charles. In the first place you couldn't call him Prince Charles. 'Sir' is the form. With the Queen it's 'Your Majesty' for openers, and then 'Ma'am' (pronounced 'Mam') as many times as you can fit in afterwards. You could ask the Prince, "How's your mother?" but you'd get a chilly response in which he would refer to her only as 'The Queen'. And someone like Princess Anne is incapable of using words like 'my', preferring the construction 'one's', as in 'one's horse'. This has the effect of implying that everyone has a horse, thus widening the distance between the Princess and the rest of the country. I am also told that it is expected, even with minor royals, that you will not speak until you are spoken to and not talk about any matter they have not raised first.

I can't offer much first-hand knowledge of these things, but even a glimpse of royal life reveals a machine so well engineered you are scarcely aware there are any moving parts. Some years ago I was among a number of journalists who went to a reception on board the Royal Yacht *Britannia*, berthed in Swansea. After a while I became aware of what the system was. Every guest on that boat had to meet the Prince in the course of an hour and a half or so. There were to be no exceptions as his staff unobtrusively steered him through the throng. You might have thought he was making his way haphazardly among a crowd of guests, talking to anyone who happened to catch his eye, but not a bit of it.

It was only because I was in the very last group in his progress that I began to realise what was going on. "Have you met the Prince?" a press officer would ask, making sure, it became apparent, that no-one was left out. But, I wondered, after three of us had had our couple of minutes, did he now believe he had met people who had told him what they really thought. I somehow got the impression that he did, and I got it again the next time I saw this process in action.

In the light of all these things you begin to wonder if it's possible for any Prince of Wales, however earnest and ostentatiously well-meaning, to have a handle on reality. It's fairly obvious, for instance, that once he's taken a line on a particular subject he's bound to find himself in the company of a lot of people who agree with him. Deference, a kind of mental walking backwards, seems to afflict even those you might normally consider to be out of sympathy with the whole circus. This may well be influential in the case of GM crops. Here the problem is exacerbated by the fact that if you've got this feeling that something's wrong, the cold eye of science tends to get pushed into the background; in particular the views of those scientists who have different opinions from yours.

In a way, though, even this argument isn't the point since opposition to experimentation with GM crops is a perfectly respectable opinion to hold. It may even turn out to be a sensible one if not, at this stage, necessarily rational. Nor does the essential point lie in the conflict between some sort of supernatural mysticism and empirical knowledge. It is, after all, only a continuation in other terms of the battle between religion and science which has gone on for centuries. No, the central question is whether Charles, however sincere his beliefs, should actually be saying anything at all.

Leaving aside his lack of formal qualifications for pronouncing on this subject, even leaving aside the complexities of his position as an environmentalist who drives an Aston Martin, we come to the matter of why anyone should take him seriously. Essentially it is because of who he is and not because of what he knows. What the Prince of Wales has to say on any given subject, even marriage, is treated as meaningful because it can be used by other people, notably newspaper editors, to promote their own particular agenda. As well as being an adherent of some kind of mysticism, he is also a sacred figure in his own right, treated as someone who speaks essential truths almost without being able to help it. Except for those times, we have to remember, when he is accused of talking like a berk, that's to say those occasions on which he disagrees with newspaper editors.

At the same time, however, the survival of the royal family in the United Kingdom is due at least in part to the fact that its most important members have devoted themselves for many years to saying nothing of any significance, whether they know something about a topic or not. The Queen Mother is much admired for the example she has set by not giving a single interview since 1923. The Duke of Edinburgh has become noted for uttering foolish thoughts from time to time, but has largely been let off by a public who treat him as someone who is both a comic foreigner (Phil the Greek) and an upper class twit, and hence inevitably prone to gaffes of various kinds. The Queen herself has, as the years have gone on, looked increasingly as though she lives entirely on acid drops but, apart from a brief reference to her *annus horribilis*, has generally been sensitive enough to spare the rest of us her thoughts on life in general.

Now, though, the Prince of Wales has crossed an important line. While it's been perfectly acceptable for the royals to talk in generalised terms about improving the world, especially the world outside the United Kingdom, the GM issue means he has become embroiled in policy. In an eccentric way he has become the champion of the average man against the faceless authoritarianism of governments and multi-national corporations.

This may be a laugh, but in a sense it represents a considerable recovery in esteem for someone who, in the period when he and his late wife were separately discussing their various adulteries on television, was probably the most unpopular man in the western world. Now he's a folk hero, at least in the pages of the *Daily Mail*.

But this is dangerous territory for a prince, especially one who in the fullness of time is expected to become a constitutional monarch. In particular because the endorsement of public opinion is not to be counted on for more than a day or two. When, for example, Prince William was pictured out fox-hunting, many people (i.e. newspapers) said his father was a disgrace for allowing it. Perhaps he agreed, because it is reported that he now numbers among his interests an enthusiasm for democracy.

It emerged in November 1999, at the time Australia held a referendum to decide whether to sever its links with the Crown and become a republic. Among other things this referendum was an object lesson in how to maintain the status quo. The alternatives were: (i) Retain the Queen as the head of state. (ii) Have a president appointed by the Australian parliament. The Australian people, recognising that they weren't being offered much of a deal here – an unnamed president for whom they would not get to vote – decided to stick with the Queen.

As a victory for monarchy this was a pretty feeble affair, but soon afterwards British newspapers reported that Charles had indicated he would be perfectly happy, in due course, to submit himself to the will of the people. As the *Sun* interpreted his views: "I want referendum like Aussies."

It seems to me that, if he really thinks this, it could well mean the end of the whole royal game. If a future monarch were to admit that he only ruled by the specifically expressed consent of the British public, rather than by right of succession, then he would already be halfway out of the door. You could be certain that if one referendum failed to get rid of him, there would be more referendums until some other result were obtained. What will surely happen in Australia sooner or later could also happen here. We must remember, it took only two goes to get a Welsh assembly, however grudging was its eventual endorsement. And that happened fewer than twenty years after the Welsh public had dismissed the whole idea with contempt.

Now it's possible that it's in the context of the assembly that the role of the Prince of Wales will be examined afresh. After all, both the Queen and the Prince, flags merrily fluttering side by side, came to open the institution. She spoke in English, he in Welsh, in an unusually emphatic attempt to demonstrate how the unity of the United Kingdom could sit easily with the distinctiveness of Wales. That at least seems to have been the idea, the political sales pitch that devolution would strengthen the Union rather than weaken it.

But for the Prince this event was scarcely more than getting another uniform out of the cupboard ("Am I an admiral today, or a general?") as he does on the other few days of the year when he goes round doing his Welsh thing. But there is now a new dispensation which asks important questions about the nature of the United Kingdom. If the power of the Welsh people is expressed within the assembly, is there now a need for a more formal representation of the Crown? On the other hand, since titles and ceremonial are out of tune with these more democratic times, is there any particular need for a prince to pop in from time to time to dish out a bit of praise and encouragement? In other words, what is a Prince of Wales *for*?

From time to time the present state of affairs is declared unsatisfactory for a variety of reasons: because Charles doesn't spend enough time in Wales, because he seems a bit loopy, because of the erratic nature of his personal life and so on. At this stage politicians and journalists with time on their hands often come up with the idea of introducing a bit more democracy into the whole system. But the truth is that Charles is Prince of Wales because he is the Queen's eldest son, and for no other reason. He is another part of the living proof that lack of democracy is what defines a monarchy – you get what you get and, except in the most extreme circumstances, you have to lump it. To talk about democracy in this context is to talk nonsense, but even Charles does so. The idea sometimes put forward that any problems that arise can be fixed by a certain amount of personnel management, such as giving the job to a different prince, is to call the whole hereditary system into question. If it can be altered, sceptics might say, perhaps it can be disposed of altogether.

It is because of such revolutionary implications, no doubt, that Tony Blair prefers not to pursue the logic of his own constitutional changes. I think that public inertia and resistance to change may be crucial in deciding whether Charles eventually becomes king or not. What seems inevitable is that even a pretty minor alteration in the scheme of things, the creation of a Welsh assembly, is bound to draw people's attention to other aspects of the system of government under which they live. And that includes the status and role of the monarch and what it implies. Prompted by one alteration, will voters be tempted to ask difficult questions about other aspects of democracy? That temptation may be all the stronger if the Prince of Wales continues to have his say, and hence influence, on matters of public policy, of which GM crops could be only one.

In the sixties, when I worked on the *Western Mail*, the automatic alternative expression for 'Wales' was 'the principality'. It was an unpopular expression with nationalists in particular, but as time went on, it was seen by many other people too as representing a kind of second-grade, somehow subservient status. Not only did it gradually get dropped, it even got banned by that great unifier, the BBC. No-one uses it these days, not even those passionate unionists, the Tories. Like everyone else they call Wales a country. It is a more significant change than it looks at first sight. Among the fascinating questions it may well raise eventually is how long it is possible to go on having a prince without having a principality.

8. Sir Tasker and Sir Geoffrey Tackle the Gender Issue

At a reception in Cardiff in the summer of 1999 I fell into conversation with one of those people who, although not well known to the public at large, is clearly a man of some influence. He is pretty much a fixture at public events, particularly cultural ones, and he seems to be on familiar terms with those who run the most important organisations in Wales. I am on quite familiar terms with him myself, actually, and we usually have some kind of conversation as we stand at the edge of one of the small social dodgem tracks on which the Taffia bump into each other night after night.

On this occasion he said to me, with a laugh: "Why does your wife want to join our club?"

I said: "I don't think it's really a question of her wanting to join it. It's more a matter of her being allowed to join it if she wanted to."

The institution we were discussing was the Cardiff and County Club, a red brick building in the shadow of the Millennium Stadium in Westgate Street in Cardiff. It's a jam roly-poly pudding kind of place, a kind of Toytown version of the establishment clubs of Pall Mall and Mayfair. Its members are in the main professional people, lawyers and accountants, some people from industry and from commerce, quite a number of them long retired, a few superannuated sportsmen and a substantial number of *quangoistes*. The one characteristic they have in common is that they are all men.

That was why the Cardiff and County, always known as the County Club, had become a matter of controversy at that time. My wife, Menna Richards, was then Managing Director of HTV Wales. Later that year she was to be appointed Controller of BBC Wales. She and some other distinguished women, including Glenys Kinnock and Eluned Morgan, both members of the European Parliament, felt it was an affront that they should be excluded by category from an organisation in which many of the most powerful people in Wales met privately;

where, no doubt, they discussed and arranged many of the significant matters of the day.

Perhaps my acquaintance didn't appreciate that there was an important question of principle involved here, not the only one in which the club has been involved in its time. I said to him, as I usually do at some stage in the many conversations I've had on this subject: "The fact is you'll have to change your attitude on this as you have had to on the question of race."

"What do you mean?"

"Well, there was a long period when there were no Jews in the club."

He was silent for a moment. "I hadn't thought about that. You're right. We haven't got many Jewish members. In fact there's only one."

I must make it absolutely clear that this is not to suggest that there was ever a deliberate policy of excluding Jews from the County Club, some kind of rule that prevented them joining. It was just curious that, when you consider the huge contribution made by Jews to commercial and civic life in Cardiff, particularly through the law, none of them was a member. As long ago as 1976, when I asked a Jewish solicitor about this striking phenomenon, he said: "You learn where not to apply."

Even so, when I have discussed this with present members of the club they say that, while it's possible there might have been something in this argument long ago, there is no truth in it now. In fact what the members of the County Club are most keen on is having an organisation composed entirely of people like themselves. It is a question of generalised rather than specific prejudice to the extent, I suspect, that they are not aware that it's prejudice at all. I suppose in the end it's the old matter of class lurking in the background.

The voting system for new members is designed to reinforce this aim. One vote against a nominee equals four votes in favour. It's not exactly a black ball system but it's likely to exclude anyone whose presence is unwelcome. On the Thursday and Friday of election week, a club member or a member of the club staff sits in the foyer with the voting book. Members identify themselves and write their names in the book to indicate that they have taken part in the ballot. The member then takes a piece of paper, completely blank, with no numbers or any other method of identification on it, and casts his vote. No-one can ever know how he has voted. Sometimes one or two of the proposers will hang around to urge the merits of their candidate on other members.

As I understand the system, though, there is a further informal process designed to protect the club from any kind of embarrassment. The ballot is begun on a Thursday lunchtime but, in the case of a contentious candidate, the votes cast will be examined on the Thursday evening, even though further voting is due to take place the following day. If lots of votes against have already been registered, the proposers are given an opportunity to withdraw their candidate before he can be rejected. It has never been known, I'm told, for that opportunity to be refused.

It's by such methods then, that the Cardiff and County Club maintains its particular character and you might argue that, as a private club, it is perfectly entitled, within the law, to run its affairs as it sees fit. In particular you might think that if a bunch of men want to belong to a men-only club that's their business and no-one else's. At the same time that might not stop you wondering about the extent to which they have adapted to modern life, even though many of them purport to run modern enterprises.

But it's not as simple as that. To my mind such arguments put forward on behalf of the club fall in the face of the fact that there are times when women are to be treated as a separate species from men, and so excluded; and times when they become an inferior sub-species of men and so are admitted, but on special terms. It's here, by the way, that I part company with the women campaigners who believe, as I understand it, that the Cardiff and County Club provides a convenient opportunity for influential men to take important decisions on public matters in the absence of influential women.

I have to say that on the few occasions I've been to the club I haven't seen much evidence of this. It's also the case that some members look as though they'd have difficulty finding their way out into the street unaided after a good lunch, never mind making a significant contribution to running the country.

More important, perhaps, is the fact that they've gone a considerable way towards undermining their own arguments. On occasions women are indeed admitted to the club for private functions, but for a long time they were not allowed to enter the premises through the front door. One woman who got under their guard and into the hallway was immediately rushed through the kitchen and down the back stairs, presumably before she could cause the premature deaths of elderly members with dicky hearts.

This all smacks of the ju-ju rituals of cartoon witch doctors, as does the fact that for some years women have been allowed to lunch at the club (accompanied by a man, naturally) on Saturdays. Does this mean that they are not women on Saturdays, or that they are invisible at the weekend? Or does it mean that the Cardiff and County Club bases its argument on matters of convenience rather than having any serious principle at stake?

In the light of all these circumstances it's easy to see why this state of affairs should attract the attention of assertive women who can spot discrimination shored up by phoney arguments at a thousand paces. Why were they not allowed to join this organisation? The obvious thing to do, which they did, was to send for an application form.

They were told there were no application forms. There were only two basic qualifications for membership. To be over the age of 18, which they were, and to be gentlemen, which they were not. It was simple enough, if not very satisfactory, and despite attempts to flourish sexual discrimination regulations at the club, as well as a certain amount of coverage in the press, it was the sort of row in which most people lose interest after a very short period. That includes the people who started the row, who in any case had better things to do with their time. They had, though, made their point.

And then a curious thing happened. Instead of simply getting on with their lamb chops and treacle sponge, some people at the county club thought the question of admitting women members should be further explored. The members' opinions might be sought, despite the fact that the views of the vast majority were perfectly predictable; perhaps because of the fact that they were perfectly predictable. This unexpected outbreak of democracy was to have explosive consequences.

The then chairman of the club was Sir Geoffrey Inkin, a former regular army colonel who had managed to make a respectable living in civilian life by chairing a series of quangos. By this time he was down to just one, the Cardiff Bay Development Corporation, the organisation responsible for the redevelopment of the city's docklands. He is big and noisy and convivial, a man who likes to adopt the character of a simple ex-officer picking his way through a sophisticated world which he doesn't quite understand. This is a disguise. Sir Geoffrey is a shrewd and able man.

Easily the most distinguished member of the county club is Sir Tasker Watkins. Not only is he a former deputy Lord Chief Justice, but the holder of the Victoria Cross, which he won as a lieutenant in Normandy in 1944. It is an act of heroism he has invariably refused to discuss. Sir Tasker, who was born in 1918, is a small man, five feet four perhaps, weighing possibly ten stone. He is, nevertheless, a formidable figure. Sir Geoffrey, sixteen years younger, is large, somewhere around six feet five and, at a guess, sixteen stone, or maybe even more. Despite this contrast it's difficult to say which of them you'd pick in a fight.

Not even Sir Geoffrey's most fervent admirers would claim he's a man particularly noted for his progressive views, but he has a healthy regard for democratic systems, something he once put to the test as the Conservative candidate in Ebbw Vale. As the argument over women members simmered quietly in the outside world, he came to the conclusion that he ought to try to discover what other people in the club thought of this matter. He described it, unsensationally enough, as 'the gender issue'.

He first floated the idea at a meeting of the club's trustees. It was, he said, something they should discuss. At least one person said that he believed the admission of women would eventually happen and it would be sensible to prepare for it over a period of time. Sir Tasker's response is reported to have been caustic. "The grave has been dug," he said. "Fill it in."

So it was clear from the outset that Sir Tasker's line was one you might expect one of Britain's most able and experienced lawyers to take. Once you begin officially considering an issue of this kind you are half way to conceding the argument. If you don't want change you should not admit that there is even the possibility of change. It's worth noting, too, that Sir Tasker is a senior figure in the rugby world, among other things president of the Welsh Rugby Union, an organisation that in the area of sexual prejudice makes the County Club look like the *Folies-Bergère*. For example, the WRU has one bar for committee members and another bar for committee members' wives.

Despite the eminence of his opponent, however, Sir Geoffrey was not deterred. At the annual general meeting that year he made a recommendation that a circular should be sent out, not asking for a yes or no vote, but to find out what members' views were. Should women ever be admitted? Should the matter be considered at all? There were a number of other related questions and they caused the biggest row ever to erupt in the sedate atmosphere of the County Club.

There were about sixty people at the meeting, the majority cheering Sir Tasker on as he and Sir Geoffrey thrashed out the argument. "It was like a Punch and Judy show," one witness said. The temperature rose. People who'd forgotten how to spell passion, never mind having experienced it for decades, began leaping up and down as disorder threatened. A vote was forced, in effect a vote to stifle loose talk of even thinking of allowing women to become members. It was passed by a big majority. When a much smaller number raised their hands in opposition, they were stared at.

"They looked menacing," one member told me. "They were saying: 'There they are, those are the guys. The guys who want to ruin the club.'"

Sir Geoffrey, who was reported to be deeply wounded by what he saw as a personal insult, discreetly resigned as chairman.

Well, people might say, what else did you expect from a group of old farts whose main objection to women was that their wives might become members and discover how many large gins they drank at lunchtime. Worse still, put a stop to the large gins. It might be a bit out of touch, but it would be an unhappily authoritarian world which forced changes in the rules to meet the questionable demands of political correctness.

But there was more to it than that. The vehemence of the opposition, not to change of course, but merely to finding out whether people might be in favour of change, was another symptom of an emotional disease that is endemic to Wales. That's the country's long and passionate love affair with the past. Behind Cool Cymru you find *Cawl* Cymru, a reheated stew made from the leftovers of another life.

To take a few examples of this in the wider Welsh world. Theatr Clwyd aspires to be Wales's national theatre and is run by Terry Hands, a man with a worldwide reputation as a director. Yet it's spent a great deal of time and effort in recent years mounting stage adaptations, complete with look-you dialogue, of Alexander Cordell's three not very good novels about what a bad time people had in Wales in the nineteenth century.

Patrick Jones's play, *Everything Must Go*, which had a brief run in the West End, is about the bleakest account you could find of contemporary life in the South Wales valleys. He looks back more than forty years for a hero, Aneurin Bevan. His view, in common with many other writers in Wales, is that the past may not have been much good, but yesterday was a lot better than today.

Ed Thomas's play and film, *House of America*, is seen as a searing indictment of the hopelessness of many lives in post-industrial South Wales. But when you strip it down, you realise it's not much more than a late twentieth century version (with a little added murder, incest, drug-taking and opencast mining) of *How Green Was My Valley*, that classic Hollywood mam 'n' mining movie which has given people around the world the wrong idea about Wales for sixty years. It's interesting that in recent years it's been revealed that Richard Llewellyn, who wrote *How Green...* was himself more than a bit of a phoney Welshman.

That sub-Ealing shocker starring Hugh Grant, *The Englishman Who Went Up a Hill, But Came Down a Mountain*, is often described in Welsh newspapers as 'acclaimed', although only someone who had entirely lost his critical faculties could acclaim this feeble and patronising film which is set, you've guessed it, in the past.

I think, too, the miasma of nostalgia that blurs the outlines of modern Wales is responsible for the revival of Max Boyce, that troubadour of a vanished world. To say this is not a way of trying to diminish the talent which has sustained an exceptionally long career in show business, but Max also seems to represent a seductive link with the past, with a Wales which was more readily understood.

Most obviously he is a reminder of that brief and astonishing flowering of Welsh rugby in the nineteen-seventies, a time we now visit like tourists at some folk museum, puzzling over the remnants of a distant culture. But there's much more to it than that. As Max warbled away about doctors' papers, the outside half factory and the rest of it, a more significant part of Welsh life was slipping into permanent oblivion. Heavy industry, which had defined much of Wales for most of two centuries, was to disappear from most people's lives almost before they realised what was happening. Between 1980 and 1990 in particular, the past was ripped out of the book. To listen to Max ten years after that was to revisit a time of certainties from an era of fluidity and constant change.

It is also for such reasons, I suppose, that the story of Tower Colliery, the last deep mine in Wales, has seized the imagination of so many people. Of course its story is a tremendous romance, the way in which the miners risked everything they had to buy the pit and keep it alive. It's been the subject of television documentaries, including one made in French, a radio play and an opera. Yes, an *opera*. Plans for a Hollywood movie are said to be at an advanced stage of discussion. But I get the feeling that there's a touch of superstition about all this attention, too. That as long as coal is wound up from Tower our past won't have been taken away from us entirely. We'll be able to see where we came from. We won't have to face the fact that in the next valley a mobile phone call centre will be the biggest employer in Merthyr Tydfil, once one of the most important industrial towns in Europe.

When it comes to a sense of the past and efforts to stay in it, the County Club fits in very snugly. It's a monument to the way the world once was, rather than what it is now. A self-perpetuating establishment of a reactionary social character, it apparently believes you can delay the arrival of the twenty-first century in Westgate Street by voting against it. Even liberal-minded people who are uneasy about some of the club's attitudes often reassure themselves of its essential harmlessness and their own semi-detached relationship with it. They might say, when asked: "Oh, I don't go there very often", or "I mainly use it for the parking." One friend, aware of the institution's public reputation, has more than once said to me: "Would you come to lunch at my fascist club?" I cannot emphasise too strongly that he intends this as a *joke*. Even so, you sometimes get a sense that it would be considered unseemly to ask difficult questions or to make a fuss in some other way. It wouldn't be very *clubby*, would it?

In itself that might not be much of a problem, but for the fact that among the members of the County Club are men who run some of the most important enterprises in Wales. More than that, they are deliberately sought after as members. Someone who arrives in Wales to run an organisation like the Welsh Development Agency will, as a matter of course, be invited to join. If you've got a club, after all, it's important that everyone who is like you should be a member. It's surprising, even a little disturbing, that such people, people whose purpose in life is to go forward, should be so passionate about maintaining such an anachronistic view of the world beyond their high windows.

As I've already said, I don't believe that there is anything particularly sinister about this, that people in this band of brothers give each other the businessman's equivalent of a funny handshake in the panelled bar. But because they are in a club together they have a kind of bond. It oils the wheels. If you're a member then it goes without saying you're a reliable bloke that, indeed, everyone knows everyone else in the place is totally reliable. Or more or less. And, in business and public life, the value of the casual social contact should never be underestimated. It's always a chance to move matters on a little, murmuring things like: "We must have a word some time about that chap Jenkins..."

Not for much longer, though. Just as the decline of manual work has changed the relationship between men and women who might have to struggle through an entire lifetime without sampling a decent bottle of claret, so a new social order will eventually force itself upon those who are essentially the spiritual heirs (and sometimes the actual heirs) of those who once owned their jobs.

The people who are coming to Wales to run important enterprises, as well as people who have risen from within Wales itself to run them, are no longer invariably gentlemen over the age of eighteen. Many of them are now women and they are not to be trifled with. It's significant, for instance, that a majority of the members of the national assembly cabinet are women. Then again, Anna Southall is director of the National Museums and Galleries of Wales. The Millennium Centre in Cardiff Bay, which should eventually be the home of Welsh National Opera, is run by Kathryn McDowell. By common consent Rachel Lomax was one of the most able permanent secretaries the Welsh Office ever had. She was promoted to one of the toughest jobs in the entire civil service, Permanent Secretary at the Department of Social Security. I have to say, too, that when I once saw Ms. Lomax actually in the County Club, leaning on the bar, smoking a cigarette, she looked perfectly at home. Of course, neither she nor any of the others I've mentioned would have been allowed in the next day when the rules of nature were firmly back in place and the world was restored to the condition God had always intended.

Much of this story of the County Club is irresistibly comic, a reminder to those of us on the outside of how absurd life can be in closed institutions, places where the rules are the rules because they are the rules. To most people it doesn't seem a notably controversial idea to ask other people their opinions on a particular question. Yet two gallant, distinguished and rational men, Sir Tasker Watkins and Sir Geoffrey Inkin, fell out over it.

Well, a lot of arguments aren't really about what they're supposed to be about. Sometimes we are confronted by a single alteration in our lives that abruptly makes us aware of how extensive have been the changes we haven't really noticed until this moment. A whole way of life was suddenly revealed as being under threat, perhaps even being in the process of disappearing. Twenty years before they'd have laughed off the idea of women being members. Now they feared it might actually happen. The modern world, which was definitely not a member, was pushing its way into the front hall of the County Club and they didn't like it one bit.

After the final game of the Rugby World Cup had been played on November 6, 1999, my wife and I looked across the Millennium Stadium to see Sir Tasker, as President of the Welsh Rugby Union, talking to the Queen. We tried to construct the conversation they were having.

"Well, I'm sure you're in need of some refreshment after that, Ma'am. I'd really like to invite you to my club, but unfortunately the rules... you understand."

"But it's a Saturday, Sir Tasker."

"Of course it is, Ma'am. In that case you'd be most welcome."

It doesn't have to be like this. A while ago six of us – three men, three women – were taken by a friend to the Harvard Club in New York. Its membership consists of alumni of one of the world's greatest universities. It is just off Fifth Avenue and it has an unmistakable feel of money and influence about it. It's the sort of place that used to feature regularly in cartoons in the *New Yorker* magazine, all leather and mahogany. You can judge its scale by the fact that we were present at the lighting-up of a sixty foot high Christmas tree – *inside* the club.

Drinks were ordered, snacks were brought. Our host sat next to his wife who was cradling a very small child in her arms. A waiter leant discreetly over her and murmured: "Anything for the baby, ma'am?"

Six of us immediately thought of Westgate Street and the County Club and of how far away it was. Three thousand miles and a hundred years.

9. Nick Uses A Rude Word

While watching television in the very early days of the national assembly I was rather surprised to hear a man refer to something called "the Government of Wales". Even more striking was the fact that the speaker was Nick Bourne, a leading Conservative in the assembly – soon enough, indeed, to be *the* Conservative leader, thanks to the adventures of Rod Richards. I knew perfectly well that Nick Bourne and his colleagues had never wanted a government of Wales or, for that matter, anything that could be mistaken for a government of Wales by a myopic pensioner several miles away on a misty night. And they'd got their wish. No-one who cares what words mean could describe as a government the grace-and-favour administration which by this stage was pottering about in Cardiff Bay. In particular, it could not do those things we associate with such an institution, like raising its own revenue or making laws, or being responsible for an army or a police force, never mind making war or signing treaties and the million and one other things that real governments do routinely. As its members were to discover, and I have already described, the assembly could move things about a bit, but not much more.

Now here we had Nick, someone who fancies himself as a bit of a tough nut, burbling away about the 'Government' of Wales. As part of the same process that had taken Wales from being a principality to a country, so it had now apparently acquired another of the pillars of nationhood. Countries have governments, the logic goes, and even the Tories, trench-diggers to a man in defence of the Union, were apparently quite happily acquiescing in this further change. Ah well, people might say, it's only a word. But how we describe ourselves can be crucial in the business of understanding what we are or where we are going. To think of Wales as being a country with a government could just be a small step down the road to becoming that very thing.

If for nothing else, you have to admire the Conservative Party for its stupendous capacity for adapting itself to the demands of real life. It is Darwinism made politics. They might not have liked the idea of an elected assembly, but after the event the Tories were shrewd enough to recognise it might nevertheless turn out to be a stroke of great good fortune.

They had been wiped out in Wales in the general election of 1997 and they were also having a bad time in local government. In Cardiff in 1995, for example, their representation had been reduced to a single seat. In such circumstances it's very difficult to avoid further decline, partly because of general gloom surrounding the party and its workers, but also because of a lack of the focus normally provided by MPs and councillors in the local party associations. The assembly changed all that, in particular because of the introduction of proportional representation, a system which normally has the same effect on the average Tory as does a crucifix on a vampire.

Their position hadn't been much restored even by the time of the first assembly elections in May 1999. They managed to win only one seat – Monmouth – under the first past the post method. But they got another eight members thanks to the list system. They might not have been popular, but they were at least visible. In one of those curious twists of fortune, it was defeat over devolution rather than victory that had saved the Conservative bacon in Wales.

In these circumstances the strategy adopted by the Tories was refreshingly uncomplicated. It was to complain about virtually everything that happened and to present themselves as members of the only group that had views separate from the various shades of nationalism they claimed to detect in all the other parties. Rod Richards, a man who can denounce ten things before breakfast and then eat three Shredded Wheat, set the tone. When circumstances compelled him to step aside, his successor as leader, Nick Bourne, proved to be even less addicted to political subtlety, as we were to see in the case of Christine Gwyther. To hear a Conservative say several times a week that what was needed was someone determined and courageous enough to fight central government, was to recognise that political life had indeed changed radically.

This particular approach, it seems to me, was one of the things that meant that the national assembly was quickly established as a fixture in the Welsh landscape. Even the Conservatives were asking how it should do things, not whether it should actually be doing them. Their endorsement of its place in the constitutional scheme of things meant that those who continued to oppose the whole idea had virtually no-one to turn to within mainstream politics.

The Tory certainty was also in contrast to the hesitancy sometimes displayed by Labour. That was understandable enough in a minority administration, I suppose, and in view of the treatment handed out to Alun Michael, perfectly sensible. In any case it was easy for the Conservatives to go round being certain about things since they were secure in the knowledge they'd never be called on to do anything about them.

But Labour had two other central problems. The first was that in the background was the flimsy popular foundation on which the assembly was built – a majority of only 6,721 in the referendum of September 1997 – and substantial evidence of public indifference when it came to the elections in 1999. These circumstances were bound to encourage caution, a concerted effort to reassure the voters that their interests, and in particular their money, were in safe hands down in Cardiff Bay. At the same time, as we've seen, in those matters to which the assembly might have been able to make a difference – a calf processing scheme, beef on the bone, GM crops, for example – the administration's initiatives usually ended in confusion and disarray. The public was presented with the spectacle of an organisation which wasn't sure what it might be able to do and which ended up not doing very much at all.

While all this was going on (or quite often *not* going on) the parties were busy preparing for the next election. Ron Davies's famous dream of 'inclusivity', to which everyone else paid lip service, took a back seat to the usual political objectives: how to get power or, if you've got it, how to hang on to it. It's because of this incorrigible tendency among politicians that for a long time seemed unlikely that a coalition, the subject of occasional heated speculation in the Welsh press, was ever likely to emerge.

After all, no-one was going in with the Tories, nor they with anyone else. Plaid Cymru would hardly want to face the electors as the party that helped Labour out of a difficulty. By the same token Labour wouldn't in any case want to be caught in the act of getting into bed with the Nats. It's true many people suspected that Mike German would have loved to have done a deal, not least because it would have made him personally more important. But it seemed likely that some of his Liberal Democrat colleagues would have rowed him out into the Bristol Channel and dropped him overboard rather than allow such a thing to happen.

It was for such reasons that many of us were taken by surprise on October 6, 2000, when Rhodri Morgan and Mike German announced that they had come to provisional arrangements over what they called "a partnership government", which included giving the Liberal Democrats two seats in the nine-strong cabinet. It was a clear recognition that, if the assembly were not to continue to be a shambles, some method of constructing a majority administration had to be attempted.

The truth of the matter was that political life was going to be conducted in the same way in Cardiff Bay as it had been for generations everywhere else. There were attempts to disguise this, in particular by the zeal with which the assembly adopted procedures specifically because they were not those of Westminster, reinforced by members' craving for politically correctness. What are called family-friendly hours, for example, simply curtail serious debate on the grounds that some members need to get home to have tea and a bed-time story with little Tommy or Blodwen. So it is that people who are free to decide their own hours are unwilling, even on a couple of days a week for a part of the year, to submit to some of the inconveniences regularly endured by the majority of normal working people.

Combined with other sprawling procedures, this means that properly structured debates on matters of policy, as distinct from an afternoon's nit-picking, are extremely rare. So it was, for example, that scrutiny of the crucial document which contained detailed Objective One proposals being submitted to the European Commission, had to be carried out in fifty minutes. Or again, as we've already seen, Alun Michael was dumped without a single backbencher being able to make any contribution to the public argument.

Even on one exceptional occasion when discussion was

allowed to run its natural course, the results were not encouraging. The climax of the Objective One row came in July 2000 with the Chancellor's announcement of the outcome of his Comprehensive Spending Review. For the assembly it had to be the climax of its first year of existence, containing as it did the most important elements in funding the future economic development of Wales. It was so important that Ieuan Wyn Jones, not a man with much of a reputation for humour until that moment, said on the radio that Gordon Brown, fearful of Welsh reaction, had postponed making the statement until the assembly had adjourned for the summer.

In fact the assembly un-adjourned itself for the occasion and not only held a plenary session ("Goodbye Tommy, goodbye Blodwen.") in the morning but found the Presiding Officer, Lord Elis-Thomas, willing to allow proceedings to go on until everyone who wanted to say something had said it. The review contained quite a lot of extra money for Wales although not, it seemed, full match funding for Objective One. Even so, those who only a few months before had been willing to fight to the last drop of blood for the cash had rather lost interest. They complained a bit, of course, but the mood was clear when one senior Plaid Cymru member murmured to me, as he passed the press gallery on his way out of the chamber: "I've got a lunch appointment".

A few gentle hours were filled with some party point-scoring, while a number of Labour and Conservative members stretched things out a bit more with a long series of facetious interventions. Then they all went home until September, or maybe even October. It was not a debate in any serious sense of the word. In these circumstances it was a bit rich for Rhodri Morgan, who after all is in a position to do something about it, to complain that assembly debates are more boring than watching paint dry. It is bad enough, I can testify, if you're paid to listen to a lot of this stuff, but what the voters make of it I dread to think.

It's not surprising, given its history, that these early problems in the assembly should have stemmed from an element of anxiety about how members *ought* to conduct themselves rather than how they wanted to do so. The result is that the institution lacks a sense of coherence and, frankly, a sense of dignity. You can see why, for example, members chose to address each other by their first names. Above all it's very non-Westminster, but it seems to me that this fake bonhomie causes more problems than it solves. In general, the members don't really like each other, between parties or within them, and a formalised informality only underlines for the public the generally understood proposition that all politicians are phoneys in one way or another.

To some extent, of course, that's true, and in nothing more obviously than the way in which they like to wear their compassion ostentatiously and unconvincingly, like a William Hague baseball cap. There's not much that better illustrates this than the Conservative approach to a new headquarters for the Welsh assembly. Entirely without blushing they announced a policy: "No new building. Spend the money on a children's hospital".

Brilliant. A highly-paid advertising copywriter might lock himself away in a health farm for an entire weekend in an effort to get those two words in the same sentence: 'children's' and 'hospital'. It's difficult to imagine a phrase more weighed down by its own hand-wringing sincerity.

When this wheeze was first put forward the cost of a new assembly building was said to be £23 million. For the sake of argument I'll stick with this figure since, thanks to the restless search for political advantage as well as something known as 'project creep'*, it's impossible to say what its assumed cost might have been at any given stage. The same problem applies to its actual cost, only more so.

Anyway, the Tories could claim that for that £23 million it would be possible to build a children's hospital. I dare say that was true, although there was a distinct absence of detailed costings in this proposal. But the basic idea was meant to be enticing: instead of assembly members parading around yet another monument to architectural vanity, babies and toddlers would be healed and restored to their grateful families. Among the inconvenient aspects of this heart-warming project which were resolutely ignored was – (i) There wouldn't actually be £23 million available since quite a lot of money would still have to be spent on improving facilities for assembly members, (ii) Where

* The inexorable rule that everything costs more than they told you it would when you agreed to the project.

would the health service get the money – millions of pounds a year – to run it? (iii) If the assembly agreed that it wanted to find £23 million pounds over a period of years to build the hospital it would hardly break the bank of existing resources. It was interesting, too, that when £46 million of public money (from the lottery Millennium Fund) was spent on building a rugby stadium, no-one suggested it should be used instead to build a children's hospital – or even, at that price, two.

Naturally everyone was in favour of the basic idea. Just try saying you're not. But it was only the Tories who presented this as an either-or decision which, when you thought about it, it clearly wasn't. In these circumstances it's difficult to think they intended it seriously, rather than as a way of hawking their well-scrubbed consciences around Wales.

At the same time there was another important argument: that was that if the Welsh public were to have any kind of confidence in the assembly, the assembly had to have confidence in itself. People naturally distrust attempts to invest bricks and mortar with symbolism, but perhaps there was a need for the institution to make a physical statement about its importance in the new scheme of things.

That was particularly significant in the context of the trepidation with which Wales seemed to approach its new condition. By that I don't simply mean the changed constitutional arrangements, but the way in which, in the space of fewer than twenty years, a whole society had been turned on its head by a process of industrial and economic change. Nowhere was that more obvious than in what had once been Tiger Bay and was now Cardiff Bay, a great port and a way of life and work swept away in under a generation.

Perhaps it was the instability of a drastically altered world, combined with an uneasy sense of impermanence about the assembly itself, that made some people reluctant to give it the solid and unmistakable form of a new building. In particular there was a fear that ostentatious display might persuade the public to question the soundness of their elected representatives who would be accused of taking the first possible opportunity to spend money on themselves. Given the record of many Welsh politicians in this regard it showed a commendable amount of self-knowledge. Certainly it might have been one of the factors that led Rhodri Morgan to intervene in the project at a late stage. The truth is that under the plumed Cavalier's hat of Rhodri's verbal dazzle he wears the iron helmet of a member of Cromwell's New Model Army.

Long after it had been decided that the assembly's headquarters should be in Cardiff Bay, some considerable time after it had been agreed that there should be a new building for the purpose, quite a while after the assembly itself had voted to go ahead with the project, Rhodri slammed the brakes on. Asked to sign a cheque for £1 million to fund the next stage of the new building, he'd suddenly noticed a big logistical flaw in the whole scheme.

The problem was this: while the elected members of the assembly and some staff were based at Crickhowell House, in the Bay, most civil servants were still accommodated in the old Welsh Office, two miles away in Cathays Park. You didn't need Rhodri's fabled intellectual brilliance to recognise that a lot of bureaucratic time might be wasted as the pen-pushers travelled slowly, by bus, between the two. Even an eye-witness account from an assembly member that some officials had been spotted reading at the bus-stop didn't convince him. This could be one of those economic black holes in which an unwary politician might disappear without trace. There was also an implication that, until this moment, no-one had been sufficiently brainy to appreciate the problem.

We could all see where Rhodri's logic was leading him as he progressed his argument. The national assembly had two buildings: one in Cardiff Bay, the other in Cathays Park. But, in a piece of uncanny symmetry, Cardiff City Council had two buildings: one in Cardiff Bay and the other in Cathays Park. Surely the answer must be..? Yes, the assembly could go to the old City Hall, in the centre of Cardiff, where Ron Davies (and quite possibly God, if you listened to supporters of the scheme) had always intended it to be. Where it would have been, indeed, if it hadn't been for an unseemly row over money between Ron, the Welsh Secretary at the relevant time, and Russell Goodway, the Labour Leader of Cardiff City Council.

Well, the intricacies of the arguments over where the assembly headquarters should be are of a limited fascination. The significant thing was that they were taking place at all, not least because they represented the traditional unwillingness of Welsh politicians to recognise that any argument is at an end until all those involved are safely dead – and sometimes not even then. What lay behind this was the continued resentment of the development of Cardiff Bay, a dispute that continued to divide politicians within the capital as well as causing a rift between Cardiff and the South Wales valleys. The fact that the central construction of the development, the barrage, was now an accomplished fact seemed to make no difference to the emotions attached to the arguments. But at least no-one could accuse them of not making decisions: they just kept making the same one, over and over again.

In the event, the City Hall solution had to be rejected for what looked like the last time. But even then the matter wasn't resolved. Why have a brand new building in the Bay, Rhodri argued, when we've got a perfectly good fairly new building there already? All that was needed was to stick up a new debating chamber on stilts in the car park at the back of Crickhowell House, a lean-to, as disrespectful critics called it. A bargain at £13.5 million and, if not exactly a monument to the vision and confidence of the people of Wales, at least meeting the requirements of frugality and good government.

Rhodri Morgan couldn't even get the Labour Party to vote for that one. When it came to it, he and his payroll vote (the Welsh Cabinet) found themselves lined up against many of their Labour colleagues and supported only by the Tories. A combination of the need to provide some much-needed status to the idea of an assembly, not to mention the real prospect of looking extremely foolish and indecisive, was enough to convince most people of the need for a new building. A final decision, which might turn out to be more final than the previous final decision, had been taken. Even now though, a cautious punter might well hesitate before putting the milk money on ever being able to peer through the windows of Lord Rogers's temple of democracy.

He would certainly not do so if he looked at the Welsh form book, which is why this protracted dispute over a building was more important than it appeared at first sight. Of course it wouldn't matter in the wider scheme of things if the assembly were to continue to meet and work in the utilitarian surroundings of Crickhowell House. Its sheer dullness was captured by the theatre director, Terry Hands, when he attended a meeting connected with the royal opening ceremony in May 1999. "Ah," he said, looking round the chamber, "birth of a nation in an underground car park". But then again, not building it wouldn't make much difference either. Even on the basis of the Rhodri Morgan master plan it would only mean saving about £10 million, over a period of years, to be spent on something more demonstrably caring. It was a tiny drop in the bucket of the Welsh budget.

But there was a deeper issue raised by this whole affair. That was the question of what kind of place Wales now was and what kind of place it wished to be. After all, a distinguished selection panel, headed by the former Prime Minister, Lord Callaghan, had met to judge the various submissions of leading architects for the design of the new building. Their decision had been announced to the usual fanfares and enthusiastic endorsements. But, we then recalled, we had been here before. A competition had been held to design an opera house for Cardiff Bay. A winning architect, Zaha Hadid, had been selected amid worldwide publicity. But her project was abandoned, at least in part because of the divisions in the Welsh establishment, political and otherwise. And then there was another architectural competition – to build a Centre for the Word in Swansea. The result? No building.

Ominously, in the autumn of 2000 fresh doubts began to emerge over the Wales Millennium Centre, the performing arts complex for the Bay which was largely a replacement for the opera house that never got built. Was it costing too much? Could sufficient money be found? Should the design be rethought? Familiar and responsible arguments were analysed as the construction machinery remained silent.

Each decision of this kind can no doubt be justified on its individual merits, but taken together they amount to a record of dithering, delay and failure of nerve. It doesn't take long to create an image of Wales as a place long on ambitious plans to make a mark in the world, but short on the determination and vitality to see that they become reality. There were plenty of respectable arguments for not building a new assembly headquarters (or an opera house, come to that) but not many for promising to do so and, at the last minute, deciding not to after all.

At the same time there may be some reason for wondering if the prolonged dispute over the assembly building might have represented more than simply the continuation of what was essentially an internal Cardiff dispute in another form. Was it another manifestation of that love affair with the past which has the old boys of the County Club afraid that the familiar world they knew and cherished is about to collapse? Perhaps there is an innate caution in Wales which causes people to move forward only tentatively because they are afraid of what they might find. The port of Cardiff had a central place in the tumultuous industrial history of Wales. To put up glittering new monuments is a public recognition of the revolution that has taken place in our lives. If we don't do that perhaps we can pretend a little that those lives haven't really been overturned, just temporarily altered.

And then, as we have seen over Objective One, there is the national tendency to gloom and despair, an addiction to pessimism which is almost religious in its character. Putting our faith in the superficialities of display will surely be met by the most terrible retribution. The grandiose fantasies of show-off architects, people who don't have to live with the consequences of their interpretation of this year's fashion, people whose homes are probably Georgian rectories, will make us look an easy touch for a smart sales pitch rather than the objects of international admiration. Swank, flash, showing-off, pretension, are the things we deplore most in the character of others and fear in our own. It'll cost too much, it won't work, no-one will use it – above all, such projects are elitist and exclusive. Assembly building or opera house, it will benefit only those who have all the advantages already.

What wasn't mentioned very much was that there had once been a time when someone had had to decide on the construction of Cardiff's civic centre, much admired and even more boasted-about, the picture postcard image of the city above any other. If, a hundred years previously, Cardiff (then a town, not yet a city), hadn't bought 59 acres of Cathays Park and built ambitiously upon it, there would have been no City Hall into which to try to put, and then not put, the assembly. When they asked the Marquis of Bute to sell them the land, the town council said their ambition was to build the most beautiful city in the country. Some of the emotion in the argument over a home for the assembly came from that history: that such a significant building was not fulfilling a proper public function was a standing reproach to everyone involved. You can bet they won't say that about Crickhowell House at the beginning of the twenty-second century.

This debate and all the other tensions and uncertainties that have emerged from the early days of devolution are much more significant taken together than they are as individual events. All these things, the making and unmaking of decisions, the promise of action and the failure to deliver it, the bluster and counter-bluster, the vendettas, the constant fanning of the embers of old arguments, the manner in which the assembly conducts its business, are not simply about politics, but about the nature of the Wales in which we now live. They add up.

The really significant thing about devolution lies not so much in what a small number of people do, as in what a lot of people now know. In its short life the national assembly has radically altered perspectives, sometimes in unexpected ways. Not long ago it would have been impossible to imagine the economic problems of Welsh farmers being subject to the public scrutiny they received in the autumn of 1999. And while the treatment of Christine Gwyther might in many ways have been deplorable, most people in Wales had actually *heard* of Christine Gwyther and had opinions about her. A new form of Welsh national debate was under way.

It's also the case that the despatch of Alun Michael represented a fierce spasm of resentment at being pushed around by forces from outside, a brief flicker of independence, perhaps: independence of *spirit*, anyway. In the public eye, particularly as represented in the media, Westminster has immediately been relegated to the inside pages, something that's caused huge resentment among MPs whose views on life turn out to be less deeply interesting than they were once led to believe. Us and Them politics, Wales v England, have become a much more partisan sporting contest, particularly when it comes to questions like Objective One funding.

The truth is the national assembly has meant that public life in Wales has, almost overnight, been turned into a national soap opera. Admittedly it has some of those famous Australian production values – a lot of dismal acting, clunking dialogue and improbable plot lines. Unpopular characters have been abruptly written out of the script, more attractive actors given bigger parts in an effort to shore up flagging ratings. Thanks to the ingenuity of the writers, though, Ron and Rod and Alun and Rhodri have become part of our lives in a way we could never have predicted, even as recently as that day in September 1997 when devolution slipped in like a burglar, through a window left narrowly ajar.

It seems to me that the most important question now raised is whether the national assembly will ever be much more than this, more than some form of cheap entertainment for the people it is intended to serve. As its members pick their way through hospital waiting lists, class sizes, industrial development and all the other preoccupations of politicians, you can be certain that their deeply considered decisions won't make much noticeable difference to the daily existence of the average man and woman driving up and down the A470. Devolution is only a somewhat different method of doing the same things in much the same ways as they've always been done. What we don't know is what impact it will have as an idea, rather than as a piece of governmental machinery; whether it will affect people's view of how they live and their place in the world as well as, perhaps, the world's view of Wales.

At the heart of this lies the question of whether the existence of an assembly can in turn lead to the creation of a critical constituency. Can we have newspapers, books, plays, broadcasting and other forms of communication which tell us in different ways about our condition. Politics is only part of an effective and accountable democratic system. It also needs cultural vigour and creative energy to give us a multiplicity of ways in which to analyse and understand it.

At the moment, as I say, it's emerged as a soap opera. It's perhaps significant that nowadays many popular newspapers make no meaningful distinction between the fictional world created on television day after day and the reality experienced by people watching it. The characters stalk a twilight zone between the concrete world and some electronic construct. There have been times, in its early days, when those who populate the National Assembly for Wales have seemed to inhabit similar territory. We'll find out soon enough whether they can make the transition in people's minds from second-rate play-acting to solid reality. How will it all turn out? some of us wonder as the daily drama unfolds on our screens and in our newspapers. Well, despite everything, this is a soap with a difference: in the end only the audience can decide.

Postscript

In more than thirty years as a journalist of one kind or another, one question above all has continued to puzzle me. How do we know what we *think* we know? The problem is that a great deal of journalism isn't a matter of describing as best you can unambiguous events that take place in your presence. In writing about politics in particular, your job is like that of a policeman, trying to assemble a coherent explanation of what happened from the clues left lying about and information provided by witnesses and trusted informants. Sometimes, however painstakingly you go about your work, you have to admit defeat and put the results of your investigation in a drawer with all those other unsolved cases.

In the context of this book, for instance, I have knocked on any number of doors in an effort to find an explanation for one of the more baffling incidents which had an important bearing on the turmoil that was to erupt in Welsh politics. Why was Rhodri Morgan not made a minister in 1997? Perhaps even the Prime Minister could not now give us the answer and if he could, he wouldn't since, despite Blair's best efforts, Rhodri has become a significant figure in the New Labour world and awarded the Blair accolade of 'good guy'.

In the same way I can only speculate on the strategy and motives that led Alun Michael to resign as First Secretary. Well, you might reasonably say, why not ask him? How can I put this politely? Would the answer I got be the correct one? This is not to suggest that Alun would deliberately lie to a questioner. It's just that politicians, like most other people, want to put themselves in the best possible light at all times and therefore their account of events is usually shaped to that end. It is also the case that what they say for public consumption is often modified by off-the-record adjustments.

And then there's Ron, the central figure in many of the events I have described in this book. Early in my researches I went to see him at Crickhowell House to discuss the question of an interview. He was by no means unsympathetic to the idea and, over a cup of tea in the members' dining room, spoke amicably about some of the personal questions that have been the subject of extensive public speculation. But we had a problem.

Understandably, he didn't want anything I wrote to be treated as some kind of official version of events, 'Ron's Story' in other words. Nor would I have wished it to be seen as any such thing. The difficulty was that if, in the course of discussion, what he had to say was in conflict with my interpretation of his account would I nevertheless feel less free to say whatever it was I believed to be the case. Once you've entered the relationship of a long interview, the subject also acquires some ownership rights, however much you, as the writer, might wish to resist that idea.

It was also around this time that I came across a description of the tensions that can arise in the process of interviewing and being interviewed. It was the book *The Journalist and the Murderer*, by Janet Malcolm, quoted in the *New York Review* by Joyce Carol Oates in April 1999.

"Even as [the writer] is worriedly striving to keep the subject talking, the subject is worriedly striving to keep the writer *listening*. The subject is Scheherazade. He lives in fear of being found uninteresting, and many of the strange things that subjects say to writers – things of almost suicidal rashness – they say out of their desperate need to keep the writer's attention riveted... The majority of stories told to journalists fail of their object. The writer ultimately tires of the subject's self-serving story, and substitutes a story of his own."

It would be foolish to apply this analysis too literally to any conversations Ron and I might have agreed to have, but I think it gives a penetrating insight into the way in which both sides contribute to the deficiencies of the interview as a method of establishing truth. Let me make it clear, therefore, that I did not interview Ron and any errors in my description and interpretation of his actions are entirely mine.

Of course I've talked to other people, in recorded interviews, and in casual conversations as events have unfolded over two years or so, off the record and on it. I talked at length to Alun Michael and Rhodri Morgan some weeks before Alun's resignation, but decided not to ask to revisit them afterwards. As in the case of Ron, I thought it best to write unencumbered by their particular versions of the drama. They are both transparently honest men, but they are also human.

Much of the information in this book is therefore a matter of public record. A lot of the rest could be discovered quickly enough by anyone with an inquisitive nature. Not even that perhaps, since politicians are people who think that a secret is only worth having if other people know you've got it. They spill information and analysis like water butts in a monsoon. As with the policeman, the important work is in trying to assemble a coherent story from seemingly disparate elements. I think it is worth doing if in the end it gives us some idea of where we go from here.

Index

AAEU 56
Andrews, Leighton 20
Arthur, Prince of Wales 119
Asquith, H.H. 89
Assinder, Bernard 61

Balsom, Denis 63
Banks, Tony 41
Best, Keith 92-94, 98
Bevan, Aneirin 90-91, 98, 138
Blaenau Gwent Council 61
Blair, Euan 45
Blair, Tony 16, 17, 20, 36, 39, 40, 41, 42-43, 44-45, 50-51, 53-54, 62, 75, 78, 79, 80-81, 83, 105, 109, 116, 130, 157
Boothroyd, Betty 24, 65
Bourne, Nick 69, 70, 86, 143, 144
Boyce, Max 139
Bracken, Brendan 90
British Broadcasting Corporation 130
British Telecom 93-94, 98
Brown, George 89
Brown, Gordon 45, 75, 76, 78, 147
Brown, Nick 42, 69, 71, 76
Burford, Earl of 117
Bystander 99

Callaghan, James 152
Campbell, Alastair 17, 25, 48
Cardiff Bay Development Corporation 104, 136
Cardiff City Council 25, 150
Cardiff and County Club 132-37, 139-40, 153
Carson, Edward 99
Catherine of Aragon 119
Chancellor, Alexander 31
Charles, Prince of Wales 118, 120-23, 125-30
Churchill, Winston 89, 101
Clifford, Max 23
Clinton, Bill 99, 101
Clinton, Hillary 99
Clwyd, Ann 37
Conservative Party 69, 70, 81, 84, 86, 92, 94, 95, 107, 110, 114, 116, 130, 143-45, 148-49, 151
Cordell, Alexander 138
Crossman, Richard 90-91, 98

Dafis, Cynog 112
Daily Mail 22-23, 86, 123, 128
Daily Telegraph 16, 57, 121
David, Wayne 48, 59,
Davies, Christina 23, 31
Davies, Gerald 11
Davies, Karl 61
Davies, Ron 13, 14-35, 36, 39, 41, 43, 46, 47, 50, 53, 57, 77, 84, 85, 103, 104, 145, 150, 155, 157-59
Dekover, Lindy 125
Development Board for Rural Wales 104
Dewar, Donald 47
Diana, Princess of Wales 124, 125

Ebstein, Richard 31
Edward I 118
Edward II 118-19
Edward V 119
Edward VII 119
Edward VIII 118, 119-20
Edward, Earl of Wessex 124-25
Edwards, Gareth 11
Elis-Thomas, Lord 65, 80, 81-82, 147
Elizabeth, the Queen Mother 127

Index

Elizabeth II 29, 108, 123-25, 126, 128, 129, 130, 142
Englishman Who Went Up a Hill, But Came Down a Mountain, The 138
European Commission 71, 146
European Union 70, 73, 74,
Evans, Gwynfor 38, 111

al Fayed, Mohamed 96-97
Felthouse, Julia 85
Ferguson, Lady Sarah 124
Financial Times 50
Fischler, Franz 70
Foot, Michael 91

Gaitskill, Hugh 101
Gaveston, Piers 119
Gaynor, Gloria 24
German, Mike 76, 146,
Glyndwr, Owain 78, 111
Goodway, Russell 25, 150
Grant, Hugh 138
Griffiths, Wyn 39, 40, 41-2,
Grigg, John 99, 100
Guardian 31, 42, 44, 96,
Gwynn, Nell 117
Gwyther, Christine 66-70, 72, 101, 144, 154

Hadid, Zahia 152
Hague, William 107, 148
Hain, Peter 14, 40, 51, 53, 58, 62, 105
Hall, Ruth 68
Hamilton, Christine 97
Hamilton, Neil 96-97
Hands, Terry 138, 152
Harrison, Lyndon 59-60
Henry II 119
Henry VII 107, 119
Henry VIII 106, 119
Hitchcock, Alfred 77
Hitchens, Peter 109

The Abolition of Britain 109
Howard, Anthony
Howarth, Shane 9
Hughes, Cledwyn 37, 92
Hughes, Lynne 32
Humphrys, John 81

Insitutue of Welsh Affairs 58
Insitutue of Welsh Governance 34
Inkin, Sir Geoffrey 136-37, 141
Isaacs, Sir Rufus 98

Jackson, Glenda 42
John, Barry 11
Jones, Elin 101
Jones, Ieuan Wyn 95, 112, 147
Jones, Jack 56
Jones, Mervyn 37
Jones, Patrick 138
 Everything Must Go 138
Jones, Vinnie 12

Kagan, Joseph 116
Kennedy, Charles 79
Kennedy, John F. 99
Kennedy, John F. Jr 31
Kinnock, Glenys 59, 61, 132
Kinnock, Neil 26, 61

Labour Party (UK) 34, 37, 38, 48, 49, 54, 55, 59, 62, 64, 75, 77, 92, 94, 95, 108, 116, 117
Labour Research 94
Land Authority for Wales 104
Lawrence, Jackie 33
Lewis, Saunders 111-12
Liberal Party 36, 37
Liberal Democrat Party 62, 79, 81, 82, 111, 114, 146
Livingstone, Ken 47
Llewellyn, Richard 138
 How Green Was My Valley 138
Lloyd George, David 36, 97-100, 101, 117, 119

Lloyd George, Margaret 99, 100
Lloyd-George, Lady Megan 36-37, 38
Lomax, Rachel 141

Major, John 107
Malcom, Janet 158
  The Journalist and the Murderer 158
Mandelson, Peter 21
Manic Street Preachers 90
Mao Zedong 56
Marconi 98
Mathias, Glyn 21
McDowell, Kathryn 141
Melvin, Cassandra 86
Michael, Alun 13, 21, 27, 28, 32, 33, 34, 35, 43, 47, 48, 50-58, 60, 61, 64, 65-66, 70, 71, 72, 74-77, 78-83, 86, 104, 111, 114, 145, 146, 154, 155, 157, 158
Middlehurst, Tom 67
Mitchell, Austin 44
Moister, Neil 94
Morgan, Eluned 59, 132
Morgan, Julie 43
Morgan, Rhodri 13, 14-15, 21, 36, 38-49, 51-57, 70, 77, 79, 82, 83, 103, 105, 111, 146, 147, 150-52, 155, 157, 158
Morgan, T.J. 47
Murphy, Paul 51, 79, 106

National Assembly 9, 20, 27, 28, 62, 65, 66, 69, 72, 78, 80, 103, 114, 115, 143, 144, 147-57
New Statesman 62
New York Review 158
New Yorker 142
News of the World 29
Newsnight 53
Nicholson, Jenny 90

Oates, Joyce Carol 158

Objective One Funding 33, 73, 74-77, 111, 114, 146-47, 153
Owen Jones, Jon 42, 78

Parker Bowles, Camilla 124
Parry, Thomas 120
Paxman, Jeremy 43
People 98
Perkins, Max 21
Philip, Duke of Edinburgh 123, 127-28
Phillips, Morgan 90-91, 98
Plaid Cymru 27, 28, 29, 33, 38, 60, 61, 62, 63-64, 65, 73, 75-77, 81, 92, 95, 103, 111-14, 120, 145-47
Prescott, John 54
Prince William 128
Princess Anne 126
Princess Margaret 124
Prys-Davies, Gwilym 37, 38

Redwood, John 85, 102, 107-09, 114
  The Death of Britain? 108-09, 114
Rhondda Cynon Taff Council 60-61
Richards, Liz 86
Richards, Menna 132
Richards, Rod 84-87, 96, 101, 143, 144, 155
Riddell, Mary 22
Roberts, Huw 14-15, 24, 26
Roddick, Winston 80
Rogers, Richard 151
Russell, Christobel 117-18
Russell, Geoffrey, 4th Baron Ampthill 117-18

Sergeant, John 14, 17-18
Shipton, Martin 30
Sianel Pedwar Cymru 110
Sinkinson, Brett 9

Smith, Godric 17
Smith, Llew 25-26,
Smith, Tim
Southall, Anna 141
Spectator 90-91
Stalin, Joseph 49
Stevenson, Frances 100
Stevenson, Jenny 100
Stringer, Shaun 61
Sun 129
Sunday Times 23

Tebbitt, Norman 95
Thatcher, Margaret 93
Thomas, Ed 138
House of America 138
Thomas, George 121-22
Thomas, Rhodri Glyn 62
Times 89, 125
Tower Colliery 139
Transport and General Workers Union 46, 56

Vale of Glamorgan Borough Council 61
Victoria I 119

Wales on Sunday 30-31, 32, 33,
Wales TUC 56
Wales Yearbook 2000 63
Watkins, Sir Tasker 136-37, 141, 142
Waugh, Auberon 91
Welsh Development Agency 104, 140
Welsh Industrial Development Advisory Board 103
Welsh Labour Party 14, 20, 21, 26, 27, 28, 33, 34, 36, 43, 47, 50, 51, 57, 58-59, 60, 61-63, 65-66, 67, 72, 81, 92, 111, 114, 145-46, 151
Welsh Office 17, 40, 46, 58, 78, 150

Welsh Rugby Union 9-10, 137
Western Mail 32, 78, 130
White, Michael 44
Wigley, Dafydd 64, 70, 73, 76, 112
Wilde, Oscar 99
Williams, Phil 77
Wilson, Harold 38, 39, 89, 116, 121
Wilson, Mary 39
Wordsworth, William 123
Wright, George 56-57

About the Author

Patrick Hannan is a writer and broadcaster who has covered public affairs in Wales for more than thirty years. During his career he has been industrial editor of the *Western Mail* and, for thirteen years, Welsh political correspondent of the BBC. As a television producer and presenter he has made documentaries for BBC2, BBC Wales and HTV. For almost two decades he has been a regular contributor to Radio 4 as a writer and presenter. He has been a newspaper columnist and contributed to a wide variety of publications. His book, *The Welsh Illusion*, was published by Seren in 1999.